TONY
PARKER

*Beyond All
of My Dreams*

with David Loriot

TRIUMPH
BOOKS

Library of Congress Cataloging-in-Publication Data available upon request.

This book is available in quantity at special discounts for your group or organization. For further information, contact:
    Triumph Books LLC
    814 North Franklin Street
    Chicago, Illinois 60610
    (312) 337-0747
    www.triumphbooks.com

Printed in U.S.A.
ISBN: 978-1-62937-930-2
Design by Patricia Frey

Photos courtesy of Tony Parker unless otherwise indicated.

Published in the French language originally under the title:
Tony Parker, au-delà de tous mes rêves
© 2019, Editions Solar, an imprint of Édi8, Paris, France.

Translated by Eleanor Tuttle and Frank Debonair for Lingorama

Contents

Introduction *v*

1. My Beginnings *1*

2. My Life in the NBA *39*

3. My Life in France *125*

4. My Life as a Businessman *187*

5. My "Private" Life *233*

Introduction

On June 10, 2019, I officially announced the end of my career as a basketball player. I had just celebrated my 37th birthday, and even though I had one year left on my contract with the Charlotte Hornets, I felt that the time had come to close the chapter—a 20-year chapter of a life that was richer and more beautiful than I could have ever imagined at the tender age of 11, when I dreamed of being an NBA player.

In 2017, after tearing the tendon of my left quad, I had major surgery and spent seven months recovering. A lot of people thought that I would never set foot on a court again. But I knew it was not possible for me to go out this way. So I fought—and I came back, at first with the Spurs, my favorite team, and then one final season in a Charlotte Hornets jersey. I signed that contract in the summer of 2018. It was my only season as a free agent in my 18-year NBA career. The Hornets had Michael Jordan, my idol, and Nicolas Batum, my friend. I had come full circle. I had not allowed the circumstances to end my career. The decision was all mine, and I made it with total peace of mind.

Throughout my 20-year professional career playing basketball, I have always had the mindset not to allow my decisions to be dictated by other people. I worked to never let difficult circumstances influence my destiny. I had to fight against stereotypes from an early age.

At 6-foot-1, I was considered too short to be a basketball player. I would make up for it with my speed and my unshakeable state of mind.

No NBA team had ever entrusted a European point guard with the keys to their game. I would only need two training sessions to convince Coach Gregg Popovich and the San Antonio Spurs staff to recruit me.

I would spend 18 years in Texas and would become the Spurs' leader. How difficult is it to combine playing both for the NBA and my country's national team? I worked hard to do both and come back over and over despite my failures. I would rally everyone and win the 2013 European basketball championship.

I owe everything to basketball. It was my favorite pastime and my greatest passion. It became my profession, and I became part of its history—maybe even the history of sports in general. Thanks to basketball, I'm now a businessman. Today I split my time between both of my countries—France and the United States.

I never could have imagined such a destiny. Not even in my wildest dreams, in my childhood bedroom in Normandy that was plastered with Michael Jordan posters. He was my idol and my inspiration, not only as a player, but also as a businessman. I have obviously worked very hard to give myself this dream life, which I want to share with you.

If you're holding this book, that means you're curious about me as a person and as a basketball player. In the following pages, I'm going to tell you my life story as simply as possible, in my words and with sincerity, that David Loriot, journalist for *L'Équipe*, patiently collected and drafted. My dear reader, I will even sometimes speak to you informally, because that's how I express myself—directly and without pretense.

However, before telling you about myself, I would like to introduce you to my universe. It consists of my loved ones, who have been helping and accompanying me for such a long time, and without whom I certainly would not be here today to tell you my story.

Tony Parker Senior, My Father

I inherited his character and passion. Originally from Chicago, my father came to Europe in the 1980s to make a career. He played in the Netherlands, Belgium, and then in France—notably in Denain, Dieppe, and Rouen. He instilled in me the winner's mentality that gave me my strength. In his approach and his way of looking at sports, he was essential to my education. He helped me to stay focused, to never let go, and to always be positive. Today he lives in Chicago, and we talk regularly.

Pamela Firestone, My Mother

My mother was a model when she met my father. Then she became a naturopath. She would make her famous grass juice every morning. With my mom it was all health, how to eat well, and how to rest and optimize my body. She was also a very curious person. I owe my interests and varied pursuits to my mom, from music to business. Today she lives in San Antonio because she didn't want to be far from us.

TJ Parker, My Younger Brother

I have a very strong relationship with my two younger brothers. Since I'm two years older than TJ (Terence Jonathan) and four years older than Pierre, I started looking after them early on. Both of them have been an incredible source of support. I couldn't dream of having better brothers. Jealousy has never come between us. They've always been the first people I would call after a big game—the people I was dying to talk to. TJ, who played with SLUC Nancy in the LNB Pro A League when the team won the championship in 2008, is now the head coach of ASVEL. He knows what he wants and is mentally strong. We are cut from the same cloth.

Pierre Parker, My Youngest Brother

Pierre turned quickly to coaching kids. He started in Texas with the 15- to 18-year-olds at San Antonio High School, then moved on to ASVEL, where he was in charge of the under 18s. Pierre has been more patient. He took a little more time to find his path in life, but now he is doing what he wants. In 2019, he finished his coaching certification. He found his way.

CHAPTER ONE
My Beginnings

I don't have memories of my early childhood. The furthest back that I can remember is being six years old. Before that, nothing! Of course, I have the pictures that my mother shows me and the stories she tells me. She says that until I was three, I was always with her. I would never let go of her. I would hold on to her hair and never wanted to leave her arms. When I was a little older, I clung to my father. I followed him everywhere. I would do all the warm-up exercises with him on the basketball court. I touched a basketball for the first time at the age of three. It was a lot bigger than I was, but apparently, I still tried to dribble. I don't remember any of it, only what I was told. But I've always liked hearing these stories.

The first clear image, my first memory, is from elementary school—in first grade, to be exact. I was six years old and in the middle of playing basketball on the playground during recess. All of a sudden, an older girl fell on my leg and bent it in half. I stayed on my hands and knees without being able to stand up. The teacher came to yell at me on the playground: "Come on, get up!"

I cried and told him that I couldn't, and he didn't believe me. I made my way home as best I could and was eventually taken to the hospital. My leg was broken—a fractured tibia.

Another image that has stayed with me, one that is also connected to my earliest memory, is when they removed my cast. My leg was so skinny compared to the other one, and I burst into tears, telling my mother that I would never be able to walk like before.

I don't have memories of the Parker family all together. I only know that things weren't going well between my parents. They divorced when I was five or six years old. We were in Gravelines, a small town in France. I have an image of my mother being terribly sad because her father had just died. I only met my grandfather once. I have no memories of him.

When I talk about these things, I realize that all of those childhood events never really affected me. I don't remember them making me sad. I probably said, "That's life!" I believe I went through those moments in my childhood with a positive attitude.

Depending on the problems or the highs and lows that punctuate my life, I have always looked for the *why*, or the reason that something happened. When I would hear my parents argue, I told myself that it was useless for them to be together. When they separated, they were straightforward.

They told us that they didn't get along, that they argued all the time, and that it was better this way. But they also told us that they loved us, and that they were going to do everything they could so we would be happy. And that's what they did. I never felt like my parents were divorced. They no longer lived together, they no longer slept together, yet they were always there. Both of them were there anytime there was something big; all of my sporting events, all of my games. I never felt nostalgic or even sad that my parents were no longer together.

I don't have any memories of my parents kissing each other. I must have seen it when I was two or three years old, but I have no recollection. And at the end of the day it's kind of strange that, growing up this way, I still wanted to get married. It hadn't affected me.

It All Began in Fécamp

I was born in Bruges, Belgium, because my father played basketball there at the time. I only lived there for three weeks because he signed with Denain, near Valenciennes, soon after I was born. My mother is Dutch, with an American passport. My father is American. When my parents divorced, my mother had problems with her papers. She couldn't get a work visa, and so she couldn't keep us. My father had one, thanks to his contract with the basketball team.

Just after they divorced, my brothers and I went to live with my father in Dieppe. That was difficult for my mother. But she wasn't far away. She lived in Fécamp and would come to see us during school vacations. Later she remarried, and we were able to see her more often. When I turned nine, my father went back to the United States for a year to find a job. Although he considered taking my brothers and me, we ended up staying with our mother. That's how I ended up in Fécamp.

I came close to never living in France and never having French nationality. I might never have played on the French national team! At the time, I was still an American citizen. I became a French citizen when I turned 14 and was selected to play for the under 16 French team. Lucien Legrand, the coach, Yvan Mainini, the president of the French Federation, and Jean-Pierre De Vincenzi, the DTN (National Technical Director), took care of all the formalities so I could obtain a passport and be eligible to play in the 1997 Europe U16 championship.

I was nine years old when I got my first basketball player's license. Before that, I played soccer and had done mountain biking. I liked cycling—my mother had signed me up in Gravelines. I started soccer when I was seven or eight years old in Dieppe. I had loved watching the 1990 World Cup on TV. Toto Schillaci for Italy made such an impression on me.

Then I discovered the NBA Finals! Michael Jordan! Magic Johnson! My father played basketball, so I was always more or less playing. But from the moment that I saw the Bulls-Lakers finals on TV in 1991, everything changed. Those are my first mental images. I decided to sign up for basketball immediately. In 1992, the Dream Team made history at the Olympics in Barcelona. The NBA exploded on the scene in France, and that was it for me.

I have a lot of good memories of our house in Fécamp on rue d'Arquais. My mother lived with us for a year, and then my father came back from the States. My mother went to live with her second husband and my father moved into the house with my brothers and me.

During the time when we lived with my mother, we would go sailing on the Ballastière lake. She would take us on picnics. We went to museums and took nature trips with her and our dog, a Saint Bernard that took up the entire trunk of a Citroen 2CV! My mother had a bohemian side—life was a bit of an adventure with her.

With my father, life was a little more structured. There was basketball, the practices and the games. He also played in Fécamp at the time. There are good memories in that house: video game nights with my brothers—TJ, who is two years younger, and Pierre, the "little one," who is four years younger than I am. We are very close. My dad worked a lot, and I often had to watch them. We cooked little things for ourselves. Nothing elaborate. Simple things like spaghetti bolognese, eggs, fish sticks. On the weekends, we treated ourselves to the pizzeria across from the house, Chez Momo, which no longer exists. My brothers and I loved it. It was our night out. The four-cheese pizza with the egg in the middle was our favorite. We had a lot of fun.

At home with my father, things were very, very strict. He instilled discipline in us. If we misbehaved, it was immediately the belt or the shoe.

I remember one day in particular. My father had left for work. In the living room, there was a trophy of a player taking a shot. My father had warned us: "I don't want you playing basketball in the living room." We had a little basket stuck to the wall over the living room door. My brothers and I started playing as soon as he left. Then one of us missed a shot. The ball landed directly on the trophy. It fell to the floor, and then—headless! There was the player taking the shot, but he no longer had a head. My brothers and I looked at each other and said, "We're dead!"

That night, when my father came back home, he was not happy. Not happy at all. He pulled our pants down, and we took a beating. That was his way of disciplining us. It wasn't easy with three boys. Afterward, we were no longer laughing about playing basketball in the living room.

With my mother, things were more freestyle. Since she didn't see us as often, she wanted to enjoy us. My father was much more serious. Even though we were focused on sports, he wanted us to take school seriously. My father spoke English at home, and I answered him in French. There were always both languages in the house. With my mother, we spoke only French. I never learned Dutch.

In the summer, there were soccer tournaments on the beach where we imagined that we were Brazilians. There was the banana float on the water. We would go swimming even if it was cold. I always loved the water and thought I was a little fish. I spent hours swimming with my brothers. Before leaving the beach, we had our own little ritual. Without fail, we would check the flag color to see what the water conditions were. If the flag wasn't red, we would go. But if it was red, we would rush in, telling ourselves that there would be strong wind and huge waves. We wore our shoes because of the pebbles, and we would go swimming in the high surf. The beach was a 20-minute walk from our house. We would walk through the entire city. These were some of the first impressions of my childhood, and I will always have a special bond with that city. Fécamp is where it all began.

My First Painful Loss

When I was 10 or 11 years old, we left for Rouen because my father had a new job at the city hall. He worked in the sports department, introducing young people in disadvantaged areas to basketball. We had great times there, too, especially because that's where I really started playing basketball seriously.

The first year was in Déville-lès-Rouen, and the second was in Mont-Saint-Aignan in the U16 French championship. These were my first really big games, my first real competitions. That's when basketball started taking over all my attention. After that, when I joined the U16 French team, followed by INSEP, it was as if I had started my professional basketball player life. Everything happened very quickly.

In Rouen, one of my teammates at the time, Lionel Rougier, had a basement that was around 160 square feet. He had a basketball hoop that wasn't too high, which was ideal for dunking. At the most, you could only play two-on-two, maybe three-on three. We would play basketball for hours on end in that basement every weekend. We liked it so much that we would play at his house even after we played our basketball club game. We played until we hurt all over, until we couldn't play anymore.

From that time, I still have a very painful memory of our defeat in the U16 French championship with Mont-Saint-

Aignan. We should have won—we had the best team. It was the first time that I lost at something, and it was also my first chance to win something with the club. I had already received individual recognition, notably with the Upper Normandy draft, but I felt at the time that nothing was as good as winning as a team.

In the semifinals, we played against ASVEL and won by five points. The final had come quickly. We told ourselves it was a sure thing, that we were going to win. In the end, Montpellier played 40 minutes of zone defense—in the under 16s! We lost by two points. I had a shot at the buzzer—a three-pointer—and I missed it. That stuck in my throat for a long time.

What affected me the most was the sadness of my teammates: Alexis Rambur, Lionel Rougier, Gaëtan Muller. We were young, but I was kind of the team's leader, the one who was supposed to lead the team to the promised land. It was hard to take. Even at 13, I really took it to heart. We also lost against Russia in the European Athletics U18 championship semifinals a few weeks later with the French national team. I told myself I was cursed. I was incredibly sad.

Today, I believe without a doubt that you have to go through adversity like that. Those hard knocks and losses really hurt when you're young, but I'm deeply convinced that the hurt was what motivated me afterward to want to win and dominate my sport with the other players of my generation. These experiences nurtured me, and that's why the 2000 Europe Junior championship title is also special for me. It was the first time I had won something, and it was already so important for me to win it. Even then, basketball was shaping my life.

MJ Was My Idol

In my room, I only had posters of Michael Jordan on my walls. No other player existed. He was my idol, my example, almost like a god. I wanted to be like him. Back then, the other kids would laugh when I mentioned it. They would say, "You're too short," "You're too skinny," or "There are no French players in the NBA! You'll never make it." I don't know why, but a voice inside my head kept saying, "Yes, I'm going to make it!"

From the time I was 12, playing in the U16 French championship one or two years ahead of certain players, I realized that I played well—and could dominate. But when I said that I wanted to go on to the NBA, they said, "You have a big head. You can't talk like that." I just had self-confidence. Jordan inspired me. I knew that in order to succeed, I needed to have a ton of self-confidence.

True, I was short, and true, it was still only a dream. But when I was 15, my dream became a real goal. That is when I enrolled at INSEP (National Institute of Sport, Expertise, and Performance), which took only the best young French players.

My mother took me there in the Citroen 2CV, the trunk packed with all of my possessions. I no longer remember what color the buildings were, but I do know the Boris Diaw and Tony Parker rooms didn't yet exist! What I do remember, however, is that it was a beautiful day when my mother dropped me off. Maybe it was a sign? But in the moment, while taking my stuff out of the trunk and getting settled in my room, I realized that it was the beginning of an adventure. My "real life" was beginning.

When I started at INSEP and had to leave my parents and my brothers at home, I told myself, "Okay, my only goal now is to make it to the NBA." It was like a vow, a commitment. Even if it meant making sacrifices. Even if it meant not partying with people my age. I didn't touch a single cigarette. I never used drugs. From the age of 15, I avoided anything that could have kept me from playing in the NBA. Everyone smoked at school. It was the cool thing to do. I said, "No, I want to play in the NBA. It's not good for me." I also stopped drinking soda. No more Coke, Fanta, or Sprite. I became very disciplined and was focused on one single goal: the NBA. I also stopped eating sweets, even though I loved them when I was young. As a child, whenever my father gave me five francs, I would spend them all on candy! The only lapse I would allow myself at times was a bit of fast food or a small pizza. I love eating. I'm a food lover—I was raised in France, after all.

I felt the pressure to succeed from a very young age. I had felt it first during the U16 European championships when I was only 14 years old. I had never felt this way before. When you're 14, it's hard to live with that constant pressure. But that pressure would never leave me. When you're the ambassador of a sport, when everyone is counting on you, when all hope rests on you, it becomes a part of who you are. Later, when I played with the San Antonio Spurs, where these high expectations were ever-present at each game, my coach, Gregg Popovich, constantly put pressure on me.

I'm really happy to have been able to have a variety of experiences throughout my childhood. My mother gave me the curiosity and the desire to discover another universe. Early on, I wanted to become familiar with the business world. With music, I went from rap to rock and then to classical. All of that is in part thanks to my mother. Even though basketball was my top priority and ultimate dream, she opened my mind to many other things so that I didn't only think about basketball. I told myself that basketball wasn't all there was to life. That really helped me to release all that pressure from a young age.

My ex-stepfather's mother was a cheese seller. Incidentally, that might have been what began refining my foodie palette. I love good food. It started then, when I had all the cheeses in the world spread out on a table in the garage. I slept in a room right above it, and obviously it made me want some. My curiosity got the best of me. I would go downstairs on the sly to try some of them. Even now, the meals that I love best consist of a cheese tray and some good wine—and nothing more.

Years later, this preference often got me into trouble with the Spurs. Every two weeks they would measure our body fat, and after three or four years, they gave up on me: "You will never have 4 or 6 percent body fat. You like eating cheese too much. But as long as you perform well on the court, we'll close our eyes."

Going to markets was another great experience from my childhood. When I was 10, I sold cheese and chicken. Chicken paid more and that meant a little more candy. I would work for two or three hours and make 20 francs. It was a fortune for me. We didn't have a lot, but I never felt it. My parents did everything so that we lived well. We never had problems or missed anything. Even if the fridge was sometimes empty, my brothers and I always found a way to be positive.

In Déville-lès-Rouen, when things started getting more serious with the first regional drafts, I saw that I was easily able to beat my opponent with a few tricks. I could already shoot a teardrop, and I was faster than everyone. The coaches realized that if I continued to make progress, combined with the weapon of my unstoppable speed, I could go very far. I told myself that I was going to take my future seriously. It was an escape route to the future.

I remember a particular game. I was 12, and we were playing against Saint-Omer. We had previously gotten killed on the court there, losing by 20 points. They had an amazing marching band, wild and insane fans—the atmosphere was awesome. Before the grudge match that we had to win by 20 points, I told everyone we could do it.

That Friday, two nights before the game, I went to the barber shop. I got a strip shaved around my head and had it inscribed with *Just Do It*, Nike's famous slogan. The sentence went all the way around my head and ended with the Nike "swoosh" logo. That Sunday, we played Saint-Omer again and won by 30 points. I played an insane game, and I told myself that I had a gift and could achieve something in this sport. That's also when I tested myself as a leader by trying to motivate everyone. I remember that my teammates had been excited before we took the court.

That Monday I went back to school quite proud of my winner's haircut. I had barely made it past the door when the principal immediately snagged me: "Come over here. No, I don't think so. You can't go to school looking like that." I had to shave off my *Just Do It*. I went to a Catholic school with nuns and all of that, so it didn't fly well. I'd had my new haircut for two days and didn't even get a picture of it.

Shooting for 50 Percent

When we talked about basketball, my father always spoke in a paternal way. He was not a coach. He never intervened with any of my coaches, never questioned their decisions about how to use me on the court. In two or three situations, of course, he gave me some advice, but he never interfered with the game. He was much more focused on my attitude. He called me out when I spoke too much to the referees, or advised me on how I should behave in order to motivate my teammates, or told me how to gain the advantage over my opponent or work on my left hand, etc. But in terms of coaching, he didn't overstep his boundary. He only said, "If you want to do this, you have to be disciplined. You can't mess up, can't party…These are the sacrifices involved. You'll have to kind of forget about your youth."

That's what I wanted to do. It wasn't restrictive for me. It was my passion, so I didn't notice the sacrifices. I never really understood that certain stars sometimes went off the rails because they felt like they hadn't enjoyed their youth. If you want to do this profession, you can't party—period. If you can't follow that rule, choose another profession. To me, your passion should come before everything, and what it takes to succeed shouldn't feel like a drawback. I never felt like something was missing. I never felt like I was missing out on anything throughout my childhood and my adolescence. It was my norm. Besides, watching my peers party all night and vomit the next day made me even less interested in that lifestyle.

Of course, I still went to a few parties during my teens. I remember one at INSEP when I was 15. It was at the end of the first year to celebrate our good season. We had finished fifth in the championship, and we had set a new INSEP record with 16 victories, a record that has never been broken. I only drank Malibu rum that night. It was the first time I'd gotten hammered. I didn't feel well the next day. I threw up, called my mom, and was a little ashamed. I left to go running for an hour in the woods, trying to flush it out, to cleanse myself—as though I felt somewhat guilty.

The maturity I had acquired early on, thanks to taking care of my little brothers because my dad was often absent, is what got me on the fast track. That's why, when I arrived at INSEP at 15, I was ready to play with guys twice my age and against teams where the players were between 25 and 30 years old. As early as my first year, I was selected for the LNB All-Star Game. I knew that I was ahead, and above all, I didn't want to ruin that. And at 17, I was ready when I signed my first professional contract with Paris.

If a game from that time stands out for me, it was the one against Bondy. Bondy was at the lead in the LNB Pro A championship, and I scored 28 points against them. Quite frankly, I dominated the game. I said to myself, "If at 15, I can play like this against these guys, I can really take this very, very far."

That game said a lot about my abilities and self-confidence. They were confirmed during my second year at INSEP. I blew everything out of the water and finished as the top Pro A scorer.

Before INSEP, one coach made an impression on me. His name was Pascal Pizan. I played for him in Déville-lès-Rouen, and then again in Mont-Saint-Aignan. He was a little like Popovich—very strict, but fair. He was good for me. He gave me free rein while keeping me from going out of control. Early on, I had rather strict coaches who emphasized efficiency: shoot with over 50 percent success and avoid taking bad shots. They made me understand that just because I had a certain talent did not mean I could allow myself to take any old shot. Bruno Suarez, who was my coach during the Haute-Normandie draft and at CERN, had the same philosophy.

Lucien Legrand was my U16 France coach, and then I played for him again during my two seasons at INSEP. He was the one who made this deal with me: "You have free rein if you shoot at 50 percent."

When you're a point guard and a scorer, it's important to be efficient. At the time, I was fighting against classic point guards. It wasn't "normal" in France for a point guard to be so aggressive. In the States, this was the norm. In France, the ideal point guard was Valéry Demory. I told myself that I couldn't waste my talent on scoring. Yet, in order to earn this "freedom" in the game, I needed to shoot over 50 percent. That way, no one could say anything. That stayed in my mind throughout my entire career. If you look at the evolution of my career, I always worked, little by little, to fuse both aspects of being a point guard—the scorer and the passer—so that I could find the middle ground.

The only coach who was somewhat different and didn't really fit the profile was Pierre Vincent. His style was more like that of Phil Jackson, the coach with 11 NBA titles (six with the Bulls and five with the Lakers). But in the end, playing for Lucien and Pierre was really beneficial for me.

Pierre gave me another outlook on basketball. He was the one who instilled in me the basics of what it was to be a real point guard. He pushed me to take my time and to not necessarily want to score everything in the first quarter. He taught me the concept of sharing and trusting my teammates. He really helped me in that sense. And he was right, because you can't win anything without your teammates.

The first time that I met Pierre Vincent was during a training period in Mont-de-Marsan. He couldn't believe his eyes. "Who is this kid?! You're fast but there's no basketball substance," he said. And that was it. For me, I was beating my opponents, and that was enough. I was caught up in duels, not strategy or creating the right situation for my teammates.

When you are a junior player at the U16 level, you just want to dominate. The person who scores the most points is the one who wins. At that age, basketball is rather basic. But I was always willing to listen. I always took criticism well. If I wanted to be one of the best in the world, I needed to be tactical and strategic.

Everything Pierre told me seemed logical. It was the other side of the game that I hadn't yet explored, and an area in which I absolutely had to progress in order to become a well-rounded player.

There were two NBA point guards that I liked at the time: Isiah Thomas and Gary Payton. They were about my size. Isiah was pretty fast, and I liked Gary's self-confidence. I started following French basketball when I was about 15 years old. Before that, I was more interested in the NBA.

My first memories are of the "Cardiac Kids" from Levallois: Mous Sonko, Thierry Zig, Sacha Giffa, Vincent Masingue. I also watched ASVEL with Delaney Rudd and Alain Digbeu, at the EuroLeague Final Four in Rome in 1997. I don't remember Limoges' European title in 1993, but later on, when I really took an interest in the history of French basketball (Dacoury, Rigaudeau, the French Team from Pau in 1996, etc.), I watched the Limoges final with Fred Forte's interception over Toni Kukoc. It was crazy defense. At any rate, the French player I liked the most while growing up was Mous Sonko. His game looked the most like mine.

I like the history of this sport. I've watched over and over all of Larry Bird's and Magic Johnson's finals, all of Jordan's games—the Detroit Pistons' 1989 and 1990 finals. I asked my father to bring the VHS tapes from the United States. When I got to the NBA in 2001, Gregg Popovich was very impressed by my NBA knowledge. I knew the history and all of the old players! I could recite all of the champions and the finals going back to 1979.

Confident, Not Arrogant

For the 1998 U18 European championship, I was two years younger than most of the players. Pierre Vincent, the manager, asked the guys to put together the team that would go on to the European championship, and my teammates didn't include me. There were 13 out of 16 that didn't want me. I was the little kid.

Maybe they didn't really like my self-assured side too much either. I'll never know. But it didn't upset me. I knew they didn't exclude me because I wasn't good enough. More than likely, it was because I was too good. Or maybe it was jealousy. In my opinion, they didn't understand. I wasn't mad about that. I never took it badly. I told myself, "They can't understand. My goals are way bigger. It's not worth it to lose my time or energy on that." In the end, Pierre Vincent still chose me for the team. But the experience was a wake-up call for me. I was going to have to make more of an effort with my teammates so that they would want to play with me.

"The important thing is to participate." I've always hated that saying. There was nothing that annoyed me more at the time while growing up in France. We were fine with finishing second, third, or fourth as long as we had put up a good fight. That was the sports mentality in France, before the men's national soccer team won the World Cup in 1998, before Teddy Riner started winning world Judo championships, and before my career took off. It was almost as if we liked losing. It was like winning wasn't a good thing.

That's probably why I must have bothered a lot of people. My confidence came across as arrogance. When I was little, people always said that I had a big head and that I had to tone it down. For me, it wasn't arrogance. I was just self-confident, and I wanted to show that it was possible to win in France.

When you're one of the first to push the boundaries, when you're a pioneer, you get a lot of criticism. That never stopped me from persevering. I was just lucky to have coaches like Lucien Legrand and Pierre Vincent, who were ready for change, ready to guide me, and to say, "You know what, that short kid, he might just take us to the top…"

In that regard, I've always been ahead of my time. Of course, my father's American culture has a lot to do with it. We've had a ton of discussions about this, and they all ended the same way: you keep going, you make progress, you stand your ground, and one day they'll understand.

When I was 14 years old, my father took my brothers and me to Chicago to meet Michael Jordan. We drove by a playground where some kids were playing. We asked them if we could play a little game against them. We wanted to test ourselves. We always had this image of Americans being so good, and I was dying to see if it was true. I always had a thing for playing, challenging, and testing.

One day many years later, I was with Ronny Turiaf at the actor Jamie Foxx's house. He has a basketball court, and his friends started teasing us: "Yeah, the NBA, it's not like us playground players. We play real basketball."

"Come on then, Ronny and I are going to show you what the NBA is," I said.

We started playing. Things got a little heated, and we started throwing some punches. Ronny went to sit down because he didn't want to risk getting hurt. I insisted: "Come on, we have to play. They talk too much."

The more baskets I scored, the more heated Jamie got: "That's the NBA! That's the NBA!"

I've always had that competitive mindset. Even with board games when I was young, I had to win and couldn't stand losing. I would go so far as to get into fights. Since I've had kids of my own, I've calmed down. I'm more flexible. Now, if I lose, I don't make a fuss. Sometimes you have to let kids win.

They Didn't Want Me at INSEP

I almost didn't make it at INSEP. I was told I was too short, I was too skinny, that I wouldn't fit in with their standard heights or the mold of a typical point guard at the time. My godfather, Jean-Pierre Staelens, was the one that made the call and threw a fit: "You're crazy. You can't not take him. He dominates the U16 championships. He's the best player of his generation, and you're not going to take him?"

As for me, I had signed with the Cholet Youth Academy and celebrated a champagne toast with both Jean-François Martin, the academy director, and Jean Galle, the president of Cholet. Yet we still agreed that if INSEP should call, I would go to INSEP. In principle, it was the same as an academy, with the academic and the basketball elements, but at INSEP, students played against adults on the weekend. That challenge appealed to me.

INSEP called a week later. Cholet was really disappointed. My mother wanted me to go to Cholet. "Too bad for INSEP," she said. "They should have taken you right away." And we celebrated with champagne, so for my mother, it was as though we had sealed the deal.

My father tipped the scales in favor of INSEP. After three years there, I would be a free agent without a contract. With an academy like Cholet, I would have been stuck there until I was 24. My mother finally gave in, and I went to INSEP. The best players were at INSEP, and for me, if the best were there, that's where I needed to be also. I wanted to prove that I was one of the best.

INSEP was a huge change for me. I left my house and my brothers. It wasn't easy. My little brother Pierre was 11, and TJ was 13. We were always together. It was strange to be away from them. Despite the excitement, when my mother drove me and then helped me with my room, I still felt heartache at the thought of not seeing them as often.

I shared a room with Mamoutou Diarra. The "old-timers" were nice to me. Diarra, David Gautier, Thomas Dubiez—they all welcomed me with open arms. I loved it. On campus I felt like I was at an American university. All of the best athletes from every sport were there, and the atmosphere was phenomenal. You become a little adult. You eat at the dining hall. You do your laundry. You find your room, and you start your life.

I had reached the first step. The work my father had done laid the groundwork for me. I was already prepared to reach my goals. At INSEP, there were a lot of temptations, but nothing could sway me. My goal was clear in my mind. I was no longer very far from the NBA.

My first year at INSEP was like living in a dream. It couldn't have gone better. I made progress every day, and I felt that I was asserting myself more and more. My body was becoming a little more adult-like, and I was lifting weights. I loved all the bus trips and card games.

We also went to some pretty unlikely cities. Each time, the atmosphere was incredible. The game in Saint-Quentin will stay with me forever. We were in the N1 League and were playing in a packed venue in front of 3,500 people.

There was a marching band. It was madness. Same thing in Rodez. We laughed the entire time, and our team morale was sky high. On top of that, we often won and set the record for the most wins. We played great. I loved it.

During my second year, since I was the best scorer in the division, I was kind of the American on the team. Each defender did everything to stop me. The local newspapers wrote, "INSEP is here with Tony Parker." Something was brewing, and things took off. Each away game was packed.

On the other hand, our home games were quite lame. Our little gym was dark and there were no bleachers. A few parents came and stayed until the end of the game. But away games were awesome. They were real games. When you're 15 or 16 years old and the crowd is going wild for you, that's real life.

With the first article published in *Basket Hebdo* and titled, "Signed, Mr. Parker," I understood that things were getting serious. My first reaction was, "I can't disappoint anyone." From that moment on, each time I would play a game, people needed to know who Tony Parker was. Disappointing them, or having them make a trip for nothing, was out of the question. It was my source of motivation. No games off. I had to show what I could do. Somewhere in the back of my mind, I also started telling myself that sooner or later a scout would be in the gym.

The first scouts I met were during the 1997 U16 European championships. A representative from Clemson University brought me a letter. It read, "No matter what happens, in four years we're taking you on." I'll remember that forever. Dennis Felton, Clemson's assistant coach, met with my father and told him, "Your son is incredible and we want to take him on!" They followed me for four years. Later on, Georgia Tech and UCLA also wanted to recruit me, and I really thought about going.

The Three Musketeers

During my second year at INSEP, I still shared my room with Mam Diarra, even with Boris Diaw and Ronny Turiaf, who would become two of my best friends, on the team. I didn't know Boris and Ronny before that, but we clicked immediately. We were the same age and from the same generation. Boris, who we called "Bobo," was different, super curious and interested in everything. We kind of took Ronny under our wing. He was a year younger than us and was really homesick for Martinique. We were the "Three Musketeers." We were always together.

Friendship happens naturally. We may not choose our family, but we can choose our friends. The three of us complement each other. We're all different. Those two guys have given me a kind of stability. Often, when I was younger,

I would play basketball and not really know who my allies were or who was on my side. There was a kind of jealousy.

When Ronny and Bobo showed up, we just clicked. I knew right away that they would always be on my side and defend me. They would never betray me. They strengthened my self-confidence. With those two, I no longer feared taking on the role of a leader.

There is love on both sides, and that has really helped us. It's a lifelong friendship. We can go two or three months without talking to each other, but as soon as we call each other, it's like we spoke yesterday. With Ronny, I only have to call him once: "Ronny, can you be there on such and such day? It's a friend's birthday."

"No problem, I'll be there!"

Nowadays, Boris is always on his boat. He's out of network every other day. I'm always surprised when I see "Boris" flash on my phone. One day, I answered, "Hey, are you sure you're not sick, Boris? What's up?" In fact, he wanted to inform me, before it got out to the press, that he had accepted the position of president at Boulogne-Billancourt, and he wanted my opinion. I was happy that he was joining the team. It was a good position for him, and when the time would come to go to meetings and make decisions for the future of French basketball, I'd have backup. I also wanted to help him with the EuroLeague. There is a second French club that is up and coming, and if it turns out to be Boris', that would be great.

During my second year at INSEP, we won fewer and fewer games. The team had gotten younger and younger, yet it was still a great year. The N1 was also stronger. The pools were gone, and all of the teams were grouped together in a classic championship format. Still, with Boris and Ronny, our chemistry was obvious on the court, just as it was in life. We could find each other with our eyes closed.

After that second year, I only told myself one thing: "The NBA is only a matter of time." I was so comfortable with Ronny and Bobo that I thought for a long time about doing another year at INSEP. At the time, I was also comfortable with my private life.

At INSEP, there is always a day at the beginning of the season where you can meet all the new students. I had gone to watch the volleyball players, because there were always pretty girls who played volleyball. When I saw Lauriane, I thought, "Ah! She's quite pretty. I must find a way to meet her…" I went to talk to her and that was that.

Lauriane was my first real relationship. We were together for six and a half years, from 1998 until 2004. During my second year in Paris, she came to live with me. She then followed me to San Antonio and experienced my first NBA title with me. We're still on good terms today, and we still talk. I will always have a special kind of affection for her. Besides, we didn't break up because we had gotten into a fight or anything like that. It's just that we met when we were so young, and we both needed some time to experience other things. How can you know? She was the first.

When we broke up, since she had left everything to come live in the States with me, I decided to help her financially until she could get back on her feet and find a job. I helped her for two years: an apartment, a car…In my eyes, she had done a lot for me, and she had been part of my rise to fame with the NBA. She had been there for me every day and helping her was the least I could do until she could find stability. Today she's a flight attendant for Air France, which is something she always wanted to do. She has a family, two daughters, and everything's going well.

For all these reasons, knowing that Lauriane would also be at INSEP for another year, I considered doing another year there for a long time. For me, at that moment, there was only one choice. I would go to Paris or stay at INSEP, even if all of the Pro A clubs wanted me.

My Life in Paris

I was 17 when I signed my first professional contract in Paris. In the end, it was a strange choice, because I went there knowing that Laurent Sciarra was the unquestioned starting point guard. I could have chosen a club where I would have immediately been a starter. In Paris, I didn't even have the same opportunity that Théo Maledon did with ASVEL. At 17, he was playing exclusively. I was playing for a club where there was already a point guard who played on the French national team. But I made this move because I was comfortable with my life. It was more of a familial and emotional choice than an athletic one at the time.

So that first year, I didn't play much behind Laurent Sciarra. I was a little frustrated, and even more so because that season in particular, the club kept me for the final of the French Basketball Cup, in which I didn't play. This stopped me from going to Mannheim for a mini-world championship with players my age. So not only did they keep me from playing in the French Basketball Cup, but they also kept me from showing the NBA scouts what I could do. I was so bummed out. I really wanted to leave. I told myself that I was going to go to college in the States. I really thought about Georgia Tech and UCLA.

That first year in Paris was difficult. It was the first real setback of my career. I was convinced that I could play. I knew that I could have had a big season at 17 years of age. But life is a matter of opportunity. Sometimes you need to get a little lucky or be in the right place at the right time. At that time, that choice didn't present me with the best opportunities for basketball, but it toughened me up. It taught me that not everything is a given. You have to earn things.

Regardless, I never grumbled, never got angry or frustrated when going to practice. Laurent Sciarra had a great season that year. He played a nice game, and I learned by watching him. I took a few things from his game. Sometimes he would yell afterward, but that was Laurent. He was very down to earth, and I have a lot of respect for him. He helped me grow that first year. He fueled my mind so that I could be mentally strong, even though we didn't talk to each other all that much. He wanted to keep his spot, which is normal. It's not like he never talked to me. People tried to pit us against each, especially in 2001 when we were in the EuroBasket together. But Laurent was fair with me.

I also put myself in our coach's shoes. Didier Dobbel had the French national team's point guard on his team, and he was having a great season. The short guy named Tony still had time to progress. Of course, Dobbel didn't have to play Laurent 38 or 39 minutes per game. What about letting him play for 30 minutes and giving me a few? But I was never hateful. I told myself, "My time will come. But if during the second year he keeps Laurent as first-string point guard, I'm definitely out." I didn't want to have a second year like that.

The Nike Hoop Summit

Scheduled between both seasons was the Nike Hoop Summit in Indianapolis. Missing that was out of the question. I warned the club, "No matter what happens, I'm going. If you want to break my contract, go ahead. I'm still going."

I had scheduled a really important meeting. All of the NBA franchises were there. That's when the Spurs came to see me for the first time. I had to show them what I was worth. Incidentally, after that, the first NBA scouts started following me. They would be there throughout my whole second year in Paris for each home game.

I traveled with my dad. We had a good time. My dad was happy to go back to the States. People were speaking English, and very fast. But I felt right at home. I felt good all week at practice and knew that I would have a great game. I wasn't ranked in the top five. Marko Popovic, the Croatian point guard, was ahead of me, even though I killed him in the youth competition. I had a feeling: "I'll show them. As soon as I get in the game, the coach won't be able to get me off the court."

When the coach let me loose, we were down by 12. But we kept coming back. I played the rest of the game and scored 20 points and had seven assists. We lost the game by one point, 98–97.

At some point, when you know you're good, you're good. It was my destiny. The whole week I knew that I was working toward this game, and I was ready. When the game began, I scored my first two or three baskets. I felt good. I was in the zone. With those first moves, I dominated Chris Duhan, Duke's point guard at the time. I attacked him and immediately challenged him. I was aggressive. I didn't waste any time. Then I did the same thing with Omar Cook. I told myself that I was going to make that night feel like an eternity for them.

When you're on the court, you forget the scouts in the bleachers, the context, all of that. You just want to win the game. Beforehand you think about it, and you know that they're there, watching and analyzing you. You have to show what you can do, but you have to do it the right way. You can't just run amok. If you rush things or try to show off, you might miss the first five shots, and then it's over. That's also the difference between the good and the great players: knowing how to be present in the moment.

My Second Year in Paris

In 2000, my second year on the team, Ron Stewart became the coach in Paris. He had been the coach for the Cardiac Kids from Levallois, a team of young players with whom he had done incredible work. Ron came to see my father.

He wanted to do the same thing he did in Levallois, and he wanted to make me the starting point guard. He said, "He'll do one year here, and he'll leave for the NBA." I said, okay, let's go! The club also gave me a huge raise.

These were my first steps in the professional world, even though I was not even an adult. I had a car in the garage which I couldn't even drive. I took the metro and the bus to see Lauriane at INSEP. I was living in Boulogne, two minutes from the Pierre-de-Coubertin gym.

Being a pro meant there were expectations on me, and I was required to achieve results. At INSEP, there wasn't any pressure. Win or lose, it wasn't a big deal. In Paris you had Charles Biétry, the president, who would burst into the locker room when things weren't going well. You had Laurent Sciarra, who put pressure on you. But we had a good group. Cyril Julian was so nice to me. We had Americans, too; Brian Howard, a unique professional who was very serious, and Chris Kind, who was having a massive season. Great guys.

The second year was a huge leap. I was now starting and had responsibilities on a professional team. I had to handle communicating with players who were older than me. I tried to be a leader, but it wasn't easy for an 18-year-old with pros who had been there for a long time. Those relationships were complicated for me for the first four or five years of my professional career. Especially since I kind of had that American mentality, where I thought the veterans were the ones who made the decisions. Not easy to deal with that when you're the little up-and-coming prodigy.

But hey, in Paris, even if the circumstances were new, I didn't really have a problem. The team was young. Mamoutou Diarra knew me well. Jean-Marc Kraidy was a little crazy and didn't care about all of that, and I had an American coach, Ron Stewart, who had put me in that position and given me those duties.

CHAPTER TWO

My Life in the NBA

In the end, during that second Parisian year, we had a good season with the group of young players. We made it to the playoffs and were eliminated by ASVEL, who had a great team. I placed third in the MVP vote. I was 18 years old.

At the time, I thought it was a good idea to do a third year in Paris, try to win the MVP award, and then think about leaving. But my agent, Mark Fleisher, called me and said, "No, you're going to put your name in the NBA draft right now. You'll be a first-round pick."

It was a strategic decision. I told myself that if I did indeed enter my name in the draft, I would be selected at the end of the first round. Meaning I'd be drafted to a good team, since the worst NBA teams from the previous season get the highest draft picks. At the time, those teams preferred to play it safe and choose players who had just graduated from American universities rather than pick a European point guard. But if I waited another year and was, for example, MVP of the French national championships, I could be drafted in the lottery and find myself on a bad team.

My father and I had studied all of that. So, I decided it was better to be drafted at the end of the first round.

Being drafted at the top really wasn't one of my goals. Not at all. Look at Frank Ntilikina. He was drafted eighth. He was a top French player and look what team he plays for. I didn't want that. Being drafted by a good team at the end of the first round gives you a couple of years to make your way, like I did in Paris after Sciarra. I know the NBA history really well. I know how it works if you're chosen at the top. It can take four years before being traded to a good team. That wasn't for me. I play basketball to win titles and didn't want to lose four or five years of my career.

Before the draft itself, I had to complete a whole series of workouts for clubs that were potentially interested in picking me. First in Seattle with the SuperSonics, who were looking for a replacement for Gary Payton. Then in Boston with the Celtics, who really wanted me and made me do a workout the night before the draft. There was Orlando, where the coach, Doc Rivers, took a liking to me, and also in the Bay Area with Golden State. These training sessions lasted at least two hours. You did all sorts of shots, in motion or still, and then you followed that up with one-on-one or two-on-two games. The franchise staff was there, often in their entirety. They analyzed everything, even your defense. Finally, they had you do a lot of strength exercises.

During 2001, I did 11 workouts for 10 different teams. That's huge. At the time, Europeans weren't popular, especially point guards. From June 10 until June 25, I traveled all around the States for practices. You're in front of the coaches, the GMs, the owners. You do a little session in the morning, then you have a little bit of time to visit the city, and you get back on a plane at 5:00 PM to go to the next city for the next practice. You have to make yourself known.

In addition to the basketball work, the Spurs even had me take a psychological test. There were a ton of questions, and a lot of different situations were discussed. They wanted to know how I would react to various things. There were very few basketball questions. Instead, they were mainly about life in general, competition, jealousy, and so on. That gave them a personality profile, and they could see if I was in tune with them or not. I never asked for the results, but they must have been good, given that they selected me.

When I was chosen 28th by San Antonio, I was so happy. For one, I knew I was landing on a good team, and two, they didn't have a point guard already. It was perfect for me. I also knew I'd only have one shot. It was make or break. Because that's the thing; when you're on a good team, you're not given the time to grow or progress. With a bad team you're given three or four years, because no matter how bad the team is, it's in their best interest to play you. When you're with a good team, if you don't play well during the first few years, you could be traded. I knew the deal and was aware of that. I had to be good immediately.

Drafted!

However, the Spurs were mistrustful of me. The first time that "Pop" saw me was in June of 2001 in Chicago. I got off the plane and immediately went to do my workout at the gym. I was tired and a little worn out from the trip. It didn't go very well. Popovich didn't like what I showed him at all and didn't even want to see me again. Luckily, RC Buford, the San Antonio Spurs general manager, insisted.

Before that second workout, it was make-or-break time. I was starting to get some buzz. Pop let himself be convinced and said okay to seeing me a second time. My second workout took place in San Antonio. At the end, Pop wasn't singing the same tune: "We'll never get him at 28. He'll get drafted before that in the top 15." San Antonio was in fifth place from the previous season and so their draft pick was at the end of the first round. He said to me, "If you're still there in the 28th spot, we're definitely grabbing you."

It was clear in that moment that I wanted to go to San Antonio, but I was afraid that Boston would pick me at 21. I didn't really want to go to Boston. Their team wasn't the best.

I got in the car after that second workout and was going to visit the city a little before going back to the airport. I called my dad and said, "Dad, I really want to play for San Antonio. I don't know why, but I love the atmosphere here. The city is nice. I spotted some apartment buildings. I think I could live here." That was one week before the draft.

I truly thought, like Pop, that Boston would pick me. The Celtics even had me do a private workout, all alone, a few days before the draft and assured me they would take me at 21. However, there were no European point guards in the NBA back then, and I think the franchises weren't willing to take a risk. I did in fact drop down to the 28th pick, and the Spurs took me.

That draft was a funny story. I was in the bleachers with my father and my agent on the night of the ceremony. Each choice is made within five minutes. When the five-minute clock started before the announcement of the 21st pick, Crissie, a woman who worked for the NBA, came to see me and was holding out a Celtics hat. She said, "Tony, Boston's going to pick you, start coming down." So I started making my way down to the stage with the Celtics hat in hand, and then with less than three minutes away from the announcement, she said, "Ah, Tony, I'm sorry. Boston changed their mind. You can go back up." What I learned after is that Boston's GM and coach wanted me, but the owner got scared: "No European point guards. It's too risky!" Instead they took Joe Forte, who played for North Carolina in college, instead of me.

I sat back down, and the Spurs managed to get me at 28. They had been trying for an hour to set up a trade and move up in the draft to get me. Pop told me that they were so happy to have me that they had thrown a wild party. It was one of the biggest parties since the Tim Duncan pick in 1997. When I called Pop a few minutes after the pick, I simply told him, "We're going to show all the others that they made a mistake by not taking me."

September 11, 2001

Before leaving for the NBA, I had to deal with a not-so-nice incident in court. Louis Nicollin, the owner of the Montpellier soccer club and an important French entrepreneur in waste management, bought the club in Paris. He wanted a huge trade compensation for me leaving, despite having already secured a considerable sum. Gregg Popovich was there at the hearing of this little 19-year-old Frenchman he had just drafted and who hadn't even played for him. A little while later, the verdict came in. I was allowed to leave without Paris getting more money.

While we were in the courtroom, the hearing was interrupted by an announcement of what had just happened in New York. It was September 11—9/11. Then, on live TV, we saw the second plane crash into the World Trade Center tower. I still managed to get the last plane back to Paris before they closed the airports. Pop was stuck in London for a week.

Summer League

When the Spurs chose me, I kind of had the impression we already knew each other. I had done two workouts with them, followed by a short lunch together, and we had discussed quite a bit. After the draft, I participated in the Summer League in Salt Lake City. Only Mike Brown, the assistant coach, was there. Pop hadn't come. It was my first game. We arrived. We warmed up, and then—I'll remember this forever—I went to see Mike Brown.

"Mike, why isn't Pop in the bleachers?"

"He's busy."

I have to admit that I was hurt. I was his team's future point guard, and the coach didn't even bother to see me play in my first Summer League game. I told myself I was going to nail it for that first game.

I scored 29 points and had eight assists. Later on, Mike Brown would tell me that after the game, he called Pop and said, "We have found our point guard for the next 15 years. You absolutely have to come see him play in Salt Lake."

The day of the next game, while I was warming up, who did I see in the bleachers? Pop! I looked at Mike Brown, satisfied, kind of smiling. "Oh, he decided to come after all." After Mike's phone call, Pop came right away and understood that he would have me play immediately, without waiting one or two seasons for me to be ready. He had to come and see me play for himself.

Everything went well that entire week in Salt Lake. I was the best point guard in the Summer League. After that, I went to the team's regular camp. That was another world. It was the start of training for the season. I met all of the older players. It was there that I saw Tim Duncan for the first time. It was impressive. I was keeping to myself in the locker room, and I saw them all arrive. I said to myself, "Wow! No kidding! There are Tim Duncan and David Robinson. I have to be ready. It's not the same. This is no longer Paris Saint-Germain. You're in the NBA now."

Obviously, I acted like it was nothing, but I was really impressed. David Robinson was my little brother's favorite player. I could still see him lifting my little brother up in the air when he came to France a few years earlier with the Nike Air Force Tour. We had wormed our way through the crowd to get autographs. Charles Barkley and Scottie Pippen were there too. We were there, wide-eyed, and we watched them play. Now I found myself sitting in the locker room with

David Robinson, in the flesh, in front of me. They spoke amongst themselves in the locker room. I didn't say anything. I watched, listened, and learned. It was the beginning of my first year.

As soon as we hit the court and the ball was bouncing, it was game on. My competitive spirit quickly took over, and I didn't care who they were in the end. In that moment, I just wanted to show that I could play in the NBA.

The most important thing for me was showing Pop and Duncan that I deserved to be there. I was aware of Duncan's doubts. When the Spurs drafted me, he said, "But why are we drafting a European point guard? We'll never win a title with a European point guard."

At the beginning of the 2000s, when you had your eye on winning titles, taking a non-American on for that position was risky. When you're the team's superstar, like Duncan was, and you draft a European point guard, it's actually *super* risky. Technically, I was their first real project. For example, when Manu Ginobili arrived at the age of 25, he had already won the EuroLeague and was an accomplished player. With me, everything remained to be seen.

I got there with my thick French accent, though thankfully I spoke English fluently and understood everything. That was a huge advantage. As a point guard, being able to easily communicate with the staff and your teammates sped up the assimilation process. At that particular time, I didn't understand all of that. I didn't understand that the Spurs had taken a huge chance with me. I told myself that they took me because they had seen that I had talent and that they were going to try to shape me to fit their needs.

Throughout my entire career, Pop would talk to me about the difference between myself and John Stockton. John, the cerebral point guard, was at one end of the spectrum, and I, the aggressive point guard, was at the other. Pop's goal was to get me closer to the middle of the spectrum. From the first day of practice, he'd say, "I know I'll never make a John Stockton out of you, but you have to become a well-rounded point guard and get closer to the middle of the spectrum." I was aware that I needed to become a real point guard and a real leader. Basketball wasn't just showdowns and beating your opponent.

San Antonio, My City

When I got to San Antonio, I felt at home right away—the air, the atmosphere. It was weird, but I felt like I was made for playing there. It's a rather strange feeling that I had from the beginning. I did indeed take an apartment in the building I had spotted during the workout, in the city's Quarry Market neighborhood. I lived there for a year. During my second year, I felt so good there that I bought a house. It was my first big purchase. I paid $700,000, which is not a lot compared to today, but at the time, it was a huge expense for me. I stayed there until 2007, and then I bought another house that was really close to where I live today in order to follow the building progress of my current house.

As early as 2004, I had bought some land and told myself that if I signed a huge contract, I would have a house built on it. I signed my huge contract in 2005—$66 million over six years. At the end of 2006, the work began, and in 2009, the house was ready. It was such a huge project that I felt compelled to live close to the house in order to oversee the construction.

The first year, during the entire regular season, Duncan didn't talk to me. He studied me, to see how I was and how I would react. The Spurs' culture was already really solid. It's not for everyone. There's a certain mentality, and not everyone can play for the Spurs. For Pop and Tim, the Spurs' way of life was really important, and the players they bring to the club must be able to fall in line.

Just before I came, there had been a great point guard, Avery Johnson, who had just left and made history with the franchise. He wasn't a great, All-Star–type of point guard, but for San Antonio, he was a great point guard. For example, he had made the shot that won them their first title in 1999. So there were a lot of hopes and expectations for the next point guard. So much so that Duncan's best friend on the team at the time, Antonio Daniels, had been chosen to take his place. The only problem was that he wasn't really a point guard; he was more of a shooting guard.

The season had begun. It was rather average. Then one day, in the middle of a return flight from Portland to play against Orlando, Pop asked me to meet him in the back of the plane.

"I'm going to make you the starting point guard," he said.

"Did you tell Duncan? Is he okay with that decision?"

I didn't want to create problems and tension with Antonio Daniels or with Tim.

"I'm going to put you in," Pop said. "I don't want to waste time. Antonio Daniels is not a point guard. You're going to be our point guard in the future. You might as well start now. It's useless to waste time. I don't care what age you are. I'm going to coach you like a 30-year-old. I'm going to yell at you and insult you, but we're going to make you grow up fast and furious. Are you ready for that? Are you ready for all of the criticism and pressure that come with being a point guard for a team that wants to play for a title?"

I was ready.

I was 19. And there you had it. I called my father right away to tell him: "I'm going to be first-string tomorrow. This is my chance. This is my opportunity to be first-string for a long time. I can't screw this up."

The next morning before practice, Pop told everyone by saying, "Tonight, Tony is starting." I swapped my gray practice jersey for a black one, the color for starters. It happened naturally, like nothing. Nothing more to it. At the time, I told myself that it would be awesome if I managed to keep that position for the entire season. I had no clue that it would last for 15 years.

My first game as a starter was against Orlando, a very good team featuring Grant Hill and Tracy McGrady. I was ready and felt good. I scored 12 points, had seven assists, and we won. I was comfortable. In the end I felt like everything was normal. In my second game, against Charlotte and All-Star point guard Baron Davis, I scored 15 points. We were off.

Except that Duncan would still not speak to me.

He didn't talk to me for the whole year. I didn't have a single lunch or dinner with him. He really studied me. He had seen so many players come and go that he might have told himself, "This European point guard is going to stay for one or two years. We'll trade him, and it will be over before we know it." When we made it to the playoffs, and the games became really tense and important, he finally spoke to me. Nothing remarkable. Just to give me a simple piece of advice on the court. Nothing outside of basketball. But he could see that I played well, that I was on fire in the series against Seattle, and he must have told himself, "Well, it might be time to talk to the little kid because he might end up staying here longer than we thought."

After that season, the following summer, he invited me to his house. You'll never forget the first time you go to the Duncans' for the rest of your life. We sat down and started talking, and I think he had actually decided to get to know me.

My First NBA Game

I will obviously remember my first NBA game for the rest of my life. It was against the Clippers, and I scored nine points. I was on the edge of the bench. After five minutes, Pop called me in. I was super surprised. Antonio Daniels was clowning around, and Pop stood up and yelled, "Tony!" I told myself, "Ah, what? Already?" I didn't expect to be called in so early, not before the second quarter.

Duncan was double-teamed and threw me the ball. I took my first three-point NBA shot and I made it. It still makes me smile today when I think that my first NBA shot was a three-pointer. In the end, I think that sums up my career. No matter what I would have chosen to do, I would have always found a way to get the job done.

If you look at my career, aside from my speed, I wasn't actually the best. But even if I wasn't tall or strong, not the prototype of the perfect point guard, not the best shooter, in critical moments when I had to make the shot and get it done, I showed up. When I needed to be good, I was never afraid. I was ready for the big time. (Except maybe during the European Cup in 2015 with the French national team. I didn't live up to my reputation. I was 33 years old, had a shoulder injury, and it was the end of my career. But before that, from the time I was young, I was there for all the important games.)

Before that first NBA game, I was excited all day. I couldn't sleep and didn't take a nap. I was excited, but I felt ready. A little like before the Hoop Summit. In the States, Americans think first impressions are really important. You often only have one single chance to leave a good impression. Each first time is crucial. When you play well in that moment, even if afterward you screw up a few games, they say to themselves, "It's okay. He'll show up again…"

I was finally fulfilling my dream. I called my friends. I spoke to Gaëtan Muller, my brothers, and my father. I didn't call too many people, but I didn't want to experience this alone. I needed to share the moment. When Pop started me, I knew I was ready. I wasn't impressed by the Staples Center, either. I had already played in Indiana's gym at the Hoop Summit. I knew what an NBA gym looked like.

Actually, the only times I had been really impressed that season were when I met my teammates at practice for the first time, and when I played against Michael Jordan. At the time, he was with the Washington Wizards. I remember it even better since I was injured during what was supposed to be our first head-to-head matchup. The second game took place in San Antonio. I was really happy but also awestruck. Suddenly I found myself playing against him—my forever idol. Throughout the entire warmup, I watched him. When the game started, even though I was on the court, I kept on watching him. Up until then I told myself, "The game has started, better start playing." At the end, I finished as the leading scorer, with 23 points, and I was so happy to have played against Jordan. Over the two seasons we would encounter each other in the NBA, I only played in two out of four possible games against him.

Hitting the Rookie Wall

Over the course of that year, I also had to face the famous rookie wall that happens in January and February. I had trouble playing back-to-back games. I was tired. My little body suffered, and I told myself I better start lifting some weights. I was skinny and weighed 163 pounds. I really buckled down and made it to 180 pounds, the weight I maintained for the rest of my career. I had gained almost 22 pounds, but it was vital. I was tired. I was taking some hits, and it was hard. Especially since, during the second season, I had to keep proving myself.

There have been so many players in the history of the NBA who had a good first season and screwed up the second. I wanted to show progress. I had a great second season. I played well, and we won the title.

From my first NBA practices, Gregg Popovich was really hard on me. "Get your head out of your ass!" He cursed a lot and said other crazy things. It wasn't easy to handle. He was nothing like my previous coaches. But at the same time, I had grown up in a family with a father who was respected and very hard on us. It was normal for me. I never had a problem with authority. I never talked back. On the contrary, I wanted to react and show him what I could do on the court. Some players are made for that. Others are not. A lot of players told me they could never play for a coach who insulted them. It didn't bother me. I always thought he was doing it for the good of the team. If sometimes I thought he was wrong, the next day we would talk about it. He was always open to discussion.

At any rate, during my rookie season, I sometimes had tears in my eyes in the shower after practice. I told myself,

"I'll never be able to satisfy this coach. He'll never be happy." All he did was push me. Push me to test my limits. But there were never limits…I took it throughout my entire career. I never broke down in front of him or the team. I sometimes went home defeated and asking myself if I really wanted to continue playing for that coach.

I never had a full-on shouting match with him and never answered in the same tone of voice as him. Never. In my mind, the coach equaled authority, and that was just how it was. What I did was take it in front of the team and then, the next day, I would go talk to him in his office. So that he could maintain his authority, for the good of the team, I never reacted like a hothead in front of everyone. The next day, in his office, I would never tell him, "You were too hard on me." I told him that I didn't agree with him on certain things. Sometimes, I would leave his office and we still didn't agree, but we continued to make progress together for the good of the team. That was our relationship.

Pop's Coaching

There's no denying it—Pop helped me a lot. It's still hard to say what my career would have been like with another coach. I think I still would have had a great career. He surely helped me to outdo myself at certain times. I think that we helped each other, and that we pushed each other. I had such a drive and desire to succeed that nothing could stop me. I would have kept going. I could see that he was much harder on me than he was on the others. Maybe it's because I was the point guard, and he knew I could take it. He had tried with other players, like Beno Udrih or Hedo Turkoglu, but it hadn't worked at all. It actually had the opposite effect. They couldn't play anymore, and the club had to trade them. He was also hard on Tim Duncan and Manu Ginobili, but not to that extent.

It sometimes bordered on abuse with me. Once we were watching film, and he was screaming at me, insisting that I reply. Actually, he was waiting for a confrontation. I didn't answer. I just looked at him. Then he kicked me out of the meeting: "Out of the room!" All because I didn't say a word. Tim stood up and came to my defense: "That's enough, Pop. It's gone too far." Pop then made everyone leave the gym, except for Tim, Manu, and me, so that we could have a talk. He explained to us, "We can't pass up this chance to win. I can't help myself, Tony. You have to be ready. That's why I'm hard on you."

That's why Pop was so good. When it came to basketball, he was in his element. But outside of it, like when we flew, he'd call me over so that we could choose the wine together. When we went to Paris with the Spurs, we made all the restaurant reservations together. He asked for my opinion on the practice schedule, if I wanted us to practice at PSG and INSEP. Outside of basketball, he was socially a very curious and cultivated person who was interested in a lot of things. He was incredibly nice. Then again, when on the court, he was intense. Not everyone could play for him. He wanted perfection but knew it was impossible to be perfect.

Mentally, I had ups and downs at times. It wasn't easy. Some days I said to myself, "What else do you want me to do? I just scored 25 points, 12 assists, and it's not enough." When Pop would congratulate me after a game, it was "Good job." Nothing more. Very quickly I adopted that attitude too. When I would score 30, 35, or 37 points, I said, "That's a good win, but now I need to focus on the next game!" It was normal. It was my job.

The times I was truly happy at the end of a game were rare. But they happened after the wins that gave us championships, after the MVP title in the NBA Finals, and all of the times when I was named an All-Star. In those instances, it was true recognition. I was among the best players in the world. Okay, when I scored 55 points in Minnesota on November 5, 2008, I admit I was more than slightly happy. It's not every day you score over 50 points in a game. I couldn't help smiling a little bit. It only happened once in my career. I even teased Tim a little bit after that game. His own top score was 53 points, and I told him that I simply wanted to beat his score.

Now that Tim, Manu, and I are no longer in San Antonio, I don't think it's the same for Pop. The relationships we created together were unique. He'll always try to come up with something else, because Pop needs to feel that kind of affectionate relationship with his players. But he'll never again experience what he built with Tim, Manu, and me.

When I was in Charlotte, he would regularly call and tell me he missed me. That was heartwarming. He would call from a restaurant and want to know why you weren't sitting in front of him to chat. It was strange.

One reason we play sports is to experience human connection. We spend more time with our teammates and coach than with our family. We really had a special relationship. The relationship between the coach and the point guard is always kind of special. I was the one who took the brunt for everyone. One day I was in the locker room and I asked him: "Pop, why do you always put me in this place (in the middle of the locker room, facing the entrance wall)? Can't I be on the side for a season?"

"No, no! I want you in front of me. That way, when I yell, I can see you!"

Pop was the one who designated all of the locker room positions in San Antonio, and he wanted me to be in front of him. I have to admit that I've taken a lot from his managerial style that is useful for me now as the manager of ASVEL.

But I will put some aside. I don't think Pop could coach like that today. With today's sensitivity, and social networks that escalate everything you say, he couldn't. He was incredibly lucky to have first found a guy like Tim, who never batted an eye, never talked back, never said anything. Same for Manu and me. In Charlotte, when our coach James Borrego (JB) would yell a tiny little bit, and the players would complain and say that the way he yelled had "gone too far," I would say, "You have no idea what too far is. He didn't even insult you or swear at you!" JB had been in San Antonio. He was Pop's assistant coach and responsible for film work. He had experienced it. Even he had gotten chewed out. As soon as there was even a one-second delay in a sequence, he got a mouthful. Pop would look at him and say, "Well, I'm going to have to find a new video coach. You're too slow!" Although tough, he always had the ability to show his love too. Honestly, he was great.

Change of Status

At the beginning of my career, there was a time when I still looked at Jordan, Kobe Bryant, Shaquille O'Neal, Scottie Pippen, and others as my idols. I watched them during the warm-up. They were on the court, and I was a few feet away from them. I was with the players that I used to watch at 3:00 AM in France when I was a kid. The players that made me dream. Yet, as soon as the game started, I only had one desire: to prove to them that I deserved to be in the NBA. There was one thing that motivated me above everything else that first year—earning my teammates' and Pop's respect and showing the other players that I could play in the NBA.

I could tell that I was experiencing things in the fast lane, but I only realized how fast everything was moving when I went back to France after my first season.

I noticed that my status had changed. I remember my first basketball camp in La Défense. A huge event had been put up together, the Nike Battleground. It was packed. For the first time, I realized the impact I had made and possibly could have on the next generation.

There were so many people. We had set up four or five courts. Afterward, we played a gala game with Yannick Noah, Marie-Jo Pérec, Bruce Bowen, Éric and Ramzy, Gad Elmaleh, and many other celebrities. It was incredible. People were actually watching. My friends told me that the first thing they did when they woke up was to watch the NBA highlights on their phones.

The fact I had succeeded so far from France undoubtedly fascinated a lot of people. I didn't fully realize it. I was far away from all of it. Yet, each time I came back to France, the wave grew bigger and bigger. The NBA was a war machine. A lot of people in France told me that I had made them want to watch basketball again for the first time since Jordan had retired. That was one of the best compliments I could have ever received.

I was kind of a pioneer. Of course, there had been other French players before me, like Tariq Abdul-Wahad and Jérôme Moïso. But they did not make an impact. No offense, but you have to admit that they didn't leave their mark on the NBA. In my case, I was starting during my first season. I was 19 years old and playing for one of the league's best teams. I'm sure that if you ask people who don't really know much about basketball who the first French NBA player was, they'll tell you it was me. Actually, I was the third. But later I became the first on other things. Everything happened so fast for me. I think that surprised a lot of people. A year and half before, I wasn't even first-string in Pro A. The craziest thing was that I didn't even feel like I was exploding.

Starting after five games, the youngest point guard in the history of an NBA starting five, with 25 points scored during my sixth game…I knew that I was doing something exceptional. I moved on quickly to the next game. Everything happened very fast. It was only during the summer, when I went back to France, that I would assess the effects.

The Simple Pleasures of the NBA

What impressed me was the huge machine of NBA franchises, the spending and the trips. When I left for San Antonio, I was only 19. I only had one truly pro year in Paris in my little apartment, with my little Renault Scenic in the garage. And then I landed in America, where they tell you, "You can buy any car you want. You can buy any house you want." The plane left at 2:00 PM. All you had to do was get on. It was impressive. The very first time I said to myself, "This is only a dream." I could completely stretch out in the plane. During my first trip from France, I traveled in economy; I wasn't going to spend $6,000 on a business class ticket. Then one week later, for a simple exhibition game, we traveled in a private jet. At the end of my first year, when I came back to France, I admit I flew business class.

There are assigned seats in the Spurs' private jet. I was next to Mark Bryant during my first year. He was so nice. Before that, I was used to carrying my own bag, my own belongings. In the NBA, you don't lift a finger. They take care of everything, right down to your toiletries bag. They ask what you like and they buy everything for you: lotions, soaps, etc. Then they put a label with your jersey number on the corresponding products. Before an away game, when you get to the airport in your car, you hand over your bag. A guy takes it, and you just get on the plane. When you get to your destination, you get off the plane. You get on the bus that is right on the tarmac, go to the hotel, get your room, and 20 minutes later someone knocks on the door and gives you your bag. It's a wild setup.

When you experience that at 19, you're like a kid in a candy store. I really tried to keep that novelty alive throughout my entire career. Today, each time I step on a private jet, it's the same enjoyment. I'm so happy and still so thankful to have the privilege to live this way. I will never be jaded by it.

Life in the NBA is incredible. It's really important to keep your feet on the ground. Most of my friends have normal lives, and thanks to them and our discussions, I've been able to preserve the novelty and not become jaded. I didn't feel dizzy, only grateful. When you grow up with little, each time you open a room service menu, choose what you want, and hear a guy knock on the door to bring your food, it's incredible. Those are the little things in a professional NBA basketball player's life, but they have kept me smiling throughout my entire career. The day I become jaded or depressed or can't be happy with my life, it will be because I have a real issue. It's not possible.

My Age Catches Up with Me

During my rookie year in the NBA, the veterans didn't have me do anything crazy. I had to get donuts on game days and a coffee for Steve Smith, and that was it. I did it the entire year, even when I was starting. I would bring about 20 donuts on game days. Honestly, it was fine. It was tradition there, and it wasn't a big deal.

After that first season, we clearly wanted to win the title in 2003. We finished first in the regular season, with a 60–22 record. In our minds, we *had* to win the title. Our team was strong. We had the season's MVP, Tim Duncan. We had to win.

Our big moment was, of course, the second round of the playoffs against the Lakers, three-time title champions. We wanted to be the team that beat them, the team that finally got them eliminated. I had a great Game 6 in Los Angeles, and we eliminated them on their home court. It was an incredible feeling to eliminate the three-time title champions. At the end of the game, we all looked at each other and understood. If we eliminated the Lakers, we were going all the way.

In the NBA Finals, we played the Nets with Jason Kidd. It was kind of a dream for me. More so at the time because there had been a lot of rumors about him potentially coming to San Antonio, and obviously it was important for me to play well against him.

For the first three games of that series, I was on cloud nine. I was even in the running for the MVP award. I was playing at a spectacular level. But my youth caught up with me. The pressure, the fact that they were talking about me, the little Frenchy, being the Finals MVP at 21 years old. It all started weighing on me.

In the following games, I wasn't as good. I learned a lot from that first final. I think those games were even useful for the rest of my career. You have to learn that when you have big games, you shouldn't worry too much about listening to the TV or reading the newspapers. My friends were excited, and I let the event take over. It was almost like I felt out of my element. I told myself that it was normal for me to be the Finals MVP at 21. It was the first time I allowed an event to have power over me, and the last three games weren't great.

Luckily, Tim kicked ass. I wasn't frustrated. I was an NBA champion at 21. I did more than my share. I was one of the top three players on the team, and I was the second-highest Spurs scorer in the playoffs.

I never could have dreamed of being an NBA champion. My dream was simply to play in the NBA and to be a good player. To think that one day I would be a champion, and, what's more, be considered for the MVP award after three games at 21 years old, was far beyond anything I could fathom.

In reality, I never dreamed of being an NBA champion. So, being one at 21 years old…Roger Federer had won Wimbledon at 22 years old, Michael Jordan had waited a very long time, until he was 28, for his first championship. It was crazy! My first title! In the moment, I didn't actually realize it. And mainly, I didn't realize how hard it was to be an NBA champion. I was one in my second year! That's why, in particular, I appreciated the 2014 title more—and even the one in 2007—than the first title. In 2003, we were crazy and reckless. I was with my friends in the locker room and we were singing, "We are the champions!" but we didn't actually appreciate it.

Later on, when you struggle and deal with losses, you realize how hard it all is. That day, I kept picturing Jordan's title celebrations in my mind. So I grabbed a big cigar and…I pretended to smoke, because I don't. I gave the cigar to my father because he loves them. All I wanted to do was open bottles of champagne, shake them up, and spray the entire locker room.

It's hard to put into words exactly what it feels like to win an NBA title. That's sports for you: unbelievable emotions, disconnected and timeless moments. When you've worked for an entire year toward one goal with your teammates and you know that 80 percent of players—in their entire career—will never know what that feels like, you feel lucky. Every basketball player in the world hopes to one day go on to the NBA and win the title. I was experiencing that at 21 years old in my second season. It's a powerful feeling.

Afterward, we ate with the entire team and then I left to celebrate with my friends. But I didn't get drunk. I felt good; I was buzzed but not drunk. Anyway, with all the titles I've won, I never got drunk. I drink a little, but once I'm buzzed, I stop because I want to enjoy the moment and remember the night. Actually, I was almost nostalgic throughout the night as I realized what we had accomplished and everything we went through to get there. Each title has its own distinction. In 2005, it was Game 7. In 2007, it was winning the Finals MVP. In 2014, it was our first title in seven years. As for the EuroBasket 2013 title with the French national team, it was something else entirely.

Ready to Leave the Spurs

After winning that first NBA champion title in 2003, I was in another dimension. We wanted to create a dynasty with the Spurs. I started creating my image. Sponsors were coming out of the woodwork. I renegotiated my contract with Nike. I was the first French NBA champion. No one had ever seen that before. I decided to hire someone to set up a strategy and really choose what I wanted to represent, the image I wanted to show, and the values I wanted to give to the kids who were watching me. I started my foundation with my mother.

When I went back to France in the summer of 2003, the EuroBasket preparation games with the French national team were incredible. Everyone was wearing my Spurs jersey—it was crazy. Actually, I think I was very disciplined about it, very organized in my mind. It was like after winning the NBA title. We had partied for two or three days, but I didn't go off the rails. One week to go wild in Ibiza. That being said, I was 21, and it would have been understandable. But I had a European championship to prepare for.

I knew people were waiting to see Tony Parker, and I needed to be ready. And my life had been settled for a really long time. No pain, no gain. I was always in the zone. I told myself that I would have plenty of time to assess and fully realize everything I had experienced the day my jersey and I retired. So, you can sit down and tell yourself that in the end, what you did wasn't that bad, right?

I was shocked at first when the rumors about Jason Kidd's arrival in San Antonio blew up in the summer of 2003. We were NBA champions, I was young, and I was only going to get better. I didn't understand why the Spurs wanted to take on a point guard. I felt that Pop was a little embarrassed:

"Yeah, well, if he comes, we'll be able to use both of you on the court."

"Yes, but I don't want to be a shooting guard. I'm too short for that position. I'm the point guard!"

In the end, it didn't happen. Jason Kidd decided to stay in New Jersey. I didn't take it well that the Spurs had considered him to strengthen the team. But that's the NBA. It's a business. At the time, Jason Kidd was the best point guard in the NBA, and if a franchise had the opportunity to get him, I could understand why it would interest them. Still, it surprised me. I said to Pop, "If Jason Kidd comes, I'm not staying. I'll leave. I understand. I'm not upset, I'm not taking it badly, but I'm surprised. I'm the team's second-highest scorer, I have an entire future before me to be Tim Duncan's right-hand man. It's a shame. I'm happy here, and I want to spend my whole career in San Antonio." In the end, I don't know what sort of impact my speech made, because Jason Kidd decided to stay in New Jersey. But if he had come, I would have moved on.

That's the NBA. Of course, you have to do your part. You have to work hard, sleep well, take care of your body, and perform well in all the games. But when you're young, luck also plays a part in the early days of your career. As long as you're not established as unbeatable, a lot of things can happen. It wasn't really until 2006 that I started to tell myself, "It's going pretty well for me. I think I'll stay here for a while."

At that time, I was established. I had a six-year contract that I had signed two years earlier. In 2004, they gave me the third-biggest contract in the franchise's history at the time. For a 22-year-old French kid, that was huge, especially coming from a Texas-based business. Texans are very careful with their money. At the time, in terms of salary, I even became the highest-paid French athlete—even higher than "Zizou." Back then, it made waves.

Again, I wasn't fazed. When I was 19, I met a banker, Stéphane Oberer, who taught me how to manage my money. He spent a lot of time explaining the precautions to take and the risks to avoid in that area. We already had a well-established plan with Stéphane and my business manager, Bill Braden, for what we were going to do with that money.

The Big Three

The year of my second NBA title, 2005, was a strange season.

I felt that I had an increasingly important place on the team. I had great playoff games and was performing well. But then in the Finals, my last two or three games weren't up to my usual level, and that image stayed in peoples' minds. Without a doubt, people had always been very hard on me in San Antonio because I was the short French guy, and a strange choice from the get-go. If we weren't winning, it was always my fault. In 2003 and 2005, even though we were NBA champions, and even though I had performed well in the playoffs, my poor performance during the last games caused people to say things like, "In the last few games, Tony's not making three-pointers. It's going to be hard to truly dominate or create a true dynasty..." I heard these objections and felt a wariness about me. But I was going to use it to my advantage.

It really motivated me. We were NBA champions for the second time, and it was the true birth of "The Big Three," with Tim Duncan and Manu Ginobili, who had really taken off and become All-Stars in 2005. Actually, I have to admit I was a little annoyed that year. Tim and Manu were chosen for the All-Star Game, which was normal. They deserved it. Yet, we had the second-best record in the NBA, and they didn't select all three of us. They clearly didn't see me as an All-Star yet. So when we won our second NBA title, and the three best players from Phoenix were selected, it was strange. Steve Nash, Shawn Marion, and Amar'e Stoudemire had the best record of the 2004–05 season at 62–20, but we beat them all the time. I really thought I would be an All-Star in 2005. I wasn't.

That whole summer, my biggest motivation when thinking about the following season was to be chosen for the All-Star Game in 2006. I wanted to be part of the best players in the NBA, and one day, I wanted to be the best point guard in the NBA. That was my goal. In 2006, I played with an incredible fierceness that I might not have ever had before. Three-quarters of the way through the season, I was leading the league in points scored in the paint, all positions combined. Me, the little 6-foot-1 guy. I scored more points in the paint than Shaquille O'Neal or Kevin Garnett. I was really determined. I was 22 years old. I had to be an All-Star. We weren't going to wait 50 years. At the time of the vote in January 2006, I was averaging 20 points per game, and it was the first time that I performed well at each game. There was a new consistency to my game during the 2005–06 season. I wanted to reach a milestone.

Working on My Shot

It was also after the 2005 Finals that I hired Chip Engelland as my shooting coach. I heard the comments about my shot, and I could feel the defense really closing in on me. I needed to improve on that for the big games.

At the time, it was a joint request with the Spurs. They were the ones who hired him. Chip had already worked with Grant Hill and Steve Kerr in the past. In the summer of 2005, I spent one month in Los Angeles with him. All we did was take shots. I changed my style a little and the position of my thumb to be more in the center of the ball, similar to how I shot a teardrop. I had to move straighter and keep my hand from moving too far back. I needed to simplify my shot to make it more fluid. After each dribble, I tended to do a kind of arch in the center before shooting, when I should have shot straight. When I would take a shot, Chip had the impression that the basket was set on a swaying ship, and that it kept moving about.

When I got to Los Angeles for my first session, he explained to me, "All we're going to do today is take shots with one hand for two hours on the free throw line and nothing else." At first I thought his methods were strange. Actually, he would remember our first session for the rest of his life. I made my first 75 free throw shots in a row with one hand. The following days were all about shooting, shooting, and more shooting.

I needed to gain consistency. I wasn't uniform. I would play a big game and, the next day, not be able to make a shot. In 2005, right after that summer when I changed my style, I felt I was making progress. I started becoming more consistent. Still, I would need time to completely master the work and the new shooting technique. It wasn't really until 2007 that I started feeling good about my shots. I gained confidence, and that opened up a new range of opportunites for me. I was able to start playing around with my shots. I was not only taking risks in one-on-one games, which had always been my strength, but I was also able to do that with my three-pointers. For that matter, 2007, 2008, and 2009 were the three seasons when I scored the most points in the NBA. In 2008, I averaged 22 points and set a record with a 55-point game. I was playing real, complete games, and above all, it was the first time I was able to score 20 points in the NBA without doing a single layup. Before, that was totally impossible for me. If I scored 20 points, it meant I had made eight layups. My offense was much more complete during those games. I worked with Chip a lot from 2006 to 2011. After that, it was more "maintenance." I was always happy to see him.

In 2006, being an All-Star was my focus. When I learned that I was chosen, I admit I was really over the moon. Two hours before they announced the results on TV, my agent called me: "You finally made it." I had worked hard for that. I celebrated it. We had a game in New York. That's where we celebrated with friends. Even though it will never replace winning a team title, at some point you also want individual recognition. In my opinion, there's nothing better except making the All-NBA first, second, and third teams.

When I got to Houston, where the All-Star Game was, it was party time for me. All the stars were there. Hollywood was there. I was working on my music album back then. Booba came. We did our stuff, and I was right in the thick of things.

But the most important time was still Sunday and the All-Star Game itself. Kobe Bryant and Kevin Garnett greeted and welcomed me to the All-Star family. It's a real community. A second family. And I was becoming part of it. It's weird, because I thought Garnett didn't like me or my team. At the time, the Spurs and his club, the Timberwolves, had a real rivalry going on. He turned out to be really nice. I'm so happy to meet NBA players outside of competitions where our only job is to thrash each other. In the locker room at the All-Star Game, I was right between Duncan, Bryant, and Garnett. I felt fantastic.

Putting on the All-Star jacket is one hell of a feeling. It gives you a real sense of pride. When I got to the locker room, seeing the All-Star jersey hanging in my locker with "West" written on it was my biggest thrill. My second-biggest thrill was receiving my ring. I didn't even know there was a different All-Star ring given every year, with the event's logo on it. They're really nice. The coats are all awesome too. I've kept them all. Being an All-Star once or twice isn't easy, but there are a lot of people who get to live it. But being chosen more than five times means you're one of the best players over a long period of time. I was an All-Star six times. I could have definitely been picked two or three times more. But the competition for guard positions in the West among Kobe Bryant, Steve Nash, Russell Westbrook, Chris Paul, and Deron Williams was really fierce. I was an All-Star six times during the golden age of point guards in the Western Conference and I'm proud of it. I think if I had been in the East, I could have been a 10-time All-Star. Especially since, with the Spurs, I had Tim Duncan before me, who had been an All-Star every year. So I had to have been really good for them to accept two players from the same team. To put that in perspective, just think that Manu Ginobili was only an All-Star twice. As far as the number of All-Star selections, my six are the second-most among Europeans in history, just after Dirk Nowitzki.

2007 NBA Finals MVP

After 2006, when I developed my game and became part of the All-Star circle, I was pumped again for the following season. The year 2007 would be particularly special for me.

Of course, that year, like each year, we had our sights set on the title. And we found ourselves in the NBA Finals again, capable of winning a third NBA championship, in my opinion. In reality, however, the real finals weren't so much against Cleveland as they were against Phoenix in the Western Conference semifinals.

It was 2–2 in the series before Game 5 in Phoenix. The night before, while we were having a quiet night in at the hotel, Pop called Tim, Manu, and me to his room, something he never did. He said, "Guys, I rarely put pressure on you like this, but this game is really, really important. If we win this game, we're NBA champions."

In his mind it was already settled. We, too, were convinced that if we won in Phoenix, we would be NBA champions. He knew it, I knew it, we all knew it. But Pop needed to say it to us. It was a very difficult series. It was very physical and tense. That was the first time he did that. The night of the game, a few minutes away from the end, I had the ball—and the game—in my hands. I broke through and threw the ball to the corner so that Bruce Bowen could take the deciding three-point shot. We won the game 88–85. Then we just looked at each other. We knew.

Of my four NBA titles, the 2007 series against Cleveland was the easiest to win, a four-game sweep. But, obviously, it's special because I was voted MVP of that series. I had two very good games. During Game 2, I scored 30 points. It was the first time I scored 30 points in an NBA Finals game. That time, my experiences in 2003 and 2005 were helpful. After that game, people were asking me one question: "Tony, can you be MVP of the Finals? And blah, blah, blah…" All of my friends called me to talk about it. But I had flipped a switch in my mind. It was a total blackout. I told them, "Guys, I don't want to talk about that or I'm hanging up." I didn't want to talk about it to anyone. I didn't want any distraction to break my concentration. I didn't read a single news article, and actually, it was from that moment on that I stopped reading any articles during the playoffs. Before, I would read everything. Since 2007, I haven't read anything.

Then it was time for Game 3. I felt that my approach and my feelings were different from 2003 and 2005. I hit a game-winning three-pointer to finish Game 4 in style 75–72 and effectively won the MVP.

Thierry Henry had come from Barcelona. He had made the trip for that game and had even brought my mother in a private jet. Like it was a taxi! That night, while we were celebrating the title, I told myself, "I can't do any better. I'm an All-Star, NBA champion, and Finals MVP." We were champions for the third time in five years, and yet I wanted us to go further still and continue to make history.

Everyone was expecting LeBron James to be named MVP. I wasn't even thinking about it. For one, I was pro-Jordan. In my opinion, he was No. 1, so I didn't really give a shit. I didn't know about the MVP award until they announced it. I had no idea beforehand because, in my mind, the Spurs belonged to Tim Duncan. I wouldn't have been surprised if the award had gone to him. Like Shaq with the Lakers—he earned it three times in a row, but Kobe Bryant would have also deserved it given his performances. Kobe was impressive, but he never won the award during the entire time he played with Shaq. I thought it would be the same for me, and that the honor would go to Tim. So I was floored when they gave it to me. It would have made sense to give it to Duncan. He was our team's top player, and I would have had no problem with that.

When I got the MVP award, I knew that I deserved it too. Besides, Duncan already had three of them, he could leave me one. Pop was proud of me. "You've come so far!" he said. We were at our peak that year. The Big Three in harmony. No ego problems and everyone on the team knew his role. That attitude, and that sense of loyalty, is the DNA of the Spurs. All throughout our careers, Manu and I never asked for anything. We were always very respectful. We always felt that it was Duncan's franchise, and that he was the star. After him, we didn't care if the order was Ginobili-Parker or Parker-Ginobili. For us it was just The Big Three. Period.

The Spurs' Boss

That trophy took me one step further, from NBA star to superstar. I became part of the very exclusive group of players that all opponents wanted to attack during each game. That's what I had wanted, and I was ready for it. I found that I was mature enough to take on the pressure.

My early career, the 2003 and 2005 Finals, the fact I wasn't chosen as an All-Star in 2005—all of this had prepared me for taking on that status one day. It also showed Pop that once Duncan started slowing down, the "little" guy behind him was ready. We never got tired of one another. In the end, it was a very military, very hierarchical system. You waited for your turn. As your time gets closer, you win more. You get used to a certain game plan and know that it works.

Then one day, it's your turn.

In 2011, Pop called me into his office. I was a little self-conscious. He had watched the 2011 EuroBasket in Lithuania and said, "Well, it's time for you to take charge of the team and become the leader that you were on the French team."

He had watched all the games. He had seen how I handled myself on the team and how I had yelled at everyone. He had seen the influence I had over the team. Basically, he told me that he wanted me to do the same thing with the Spurs. At that moment, just like 10 years earlier in the private jet in 2001, my first question remained the same: "Does Tim agree?"

"Don't worry about Tim. He's fine. He likes you. There's no problem. But it's time for you to make your mark on this team."

I listened to him. I wasn't expecting any of that. I had just come out of a great EuroBasket tournament. It was the best one I'd had with the French national team, on and off the court. I felt ready. I was honored. The Spurs were one of the best franchises in history, and I was being asked to be their boss on the court.

During the 2011–12 season, I was the only All-Star on the team. I set the franchise's record for assists, surpassing Avery Johnson. Above all, I finished every game that season and had the ball in my hands in the fourth quarter, whereas before it had been Tim and Manu who finished and who were key players at the end of the game. Pop gave me more plays in the fourth quarter, not necessarily to score but to create opportunities for others.

Starting in 2011, I knew how I was going to play. I concentrated less on myself and my game and more on my teammates and how I could help them be better. I took the compliments we received for our game personally, particularly during our last championship title in 2014, because the way we played basketball during those three years was based on my own game, before I passed the baton to Kawhi Leonard in 2015. The process of control, sharing, and involving everyone had always been something Pop and the Spurs wanted.

It had started for me with the French national team in 2009, when the coach, Vincent Collet, asked me to change up my game a little, to set up my teammates in the first three quarters before taking the game over myself in the last quarter. I had even more pressure and responsibility on the court. It was my team, and we were going to go as far as I could take them.

I was 27 years old. It was also at that time that I hired a personal chef, Cliff. I had to be ready for all of the games, and I had to be even more careful with what I ate. I was already careful before, but I was younger then and knew that I would "burn it off" quickly. At that point, I told myself everything had to be done perfectly.

In San Antonio, Tim and I didn't really talk about it. It happened naturally. Beginning with the "handoff" season in 2011, I spoke more often in the locker room, whereas before I didn't say much. Actually, it was like my experience with the national team had simply been relocated to Texas. I stood up in the middle of the locker room and spoke. I felt comfortable. I had known my teammates for a long time. I knew that Tim and Manu supported me.

That's also when I started taking the tablet during timeouts. While the coaches talked to each other, I sat on Pop's chair and showed them what we were going to do. When we were in deep shit, my teammates started looking to me, the same way it happened on the French national team. That's when you can't screw up. It's the ultimate respect you can get as a basketball player. When the entire team looks at you and trusts you. It's an incredible feeling.

Pop was proud. It's what he had expected from me. Sometimes, when he wanted to call out a play from the sideline, like he did all the time, I shook my head no as I raised the ball: "I got it. This one's for me. No problem." He would sit back down in his chair. I never would have done that early on in my career. From that point on, it happened half the time. I was managing the team, and it was his dream. One day, he told me as much, verbatim, in his office: "My dream is to stay on my chair, have nothing to do, and watch you handle it." He was still hard on me, but in regards to our relationship, it was nothing compared to the early years.

The Worst Loss of My Career

At the time, I felt I was at my peak. I was in my prime. I was playing the best basketball I could and had been put in charge of the team. All that was left was the ultimate reward: winning a title and being able to say it was my franchise.

That's what we did in 2014. But before that, there was a huge disappointment.

In 2013, we lost to the Miami Heat in Game 7 of the NBA Finals. It was the worst loss of my career. I had never experienced something like that.

The night of Game 6, one we lost in overtime under unbelievable circumstances, we were at a restaurant with the staff, the players, and our families. The atmosphere tanked. The silence hung heavy. It was horrible. Yet, we still had Game 7 to play—a clincher. No one was champion yet. We all knew that it would be hard to overcome what we had just experienced.

We'd had a five-point lead with 28 seconds left on the clock. We were going to be NBA champions again...and then we lost. That night, at the restaurant, I felt that it was over. I couldn't speak for the others, for my teammates or for Pop, but I told myself: "This is not our year. The basketball gods are not with us. It's over." I could see the dejection on my teammates' faces. It was really hard to take. We led the series 2–1, and then at 3–2. We had the championship in our hands. It was ours. The loss was unbearable.

Twenty-eight seconds remained in regulation. We asked for a timeout. All we had to do was finish the game, and we were well known for finishing well. We were confident. We told ourselves we had to take clear shots. We needed a defensive stop, to snag a rebound, and it would be over.

I was a little euphoric. Just before, I hit a little step-back on LeBron James, then a steal and a short jump shot. In my mind, it was perfect. We were NBA champions. I might even be MVP in the Finals for the second time. I could imagine the entire scene. I could see them setting up the rope. I could see the trophy out of the corner of my eye.

Then, in one fell swoop, it gets away from you. Just like that.

Kawhi Leonard missed a shot. Manu did too. We couldn't manage to get rebounds. Chris Bosh took the offensive rebound on LeBron James' missed shot. Then he passed the ball to Ray Allen, who made the three-point shot from the corner that tied things up. Meanwhile, I was running toward him like a madman while trying not to be on him too much either. I couldn't risk the foul and losing the game before overtime. He still made a crazy shot. Even though we had Game 7 to play, Game 6 showed us it was done.

It's hard, but when I think back on it today, I tell myself I wouldn't actually change anything. The satisfaction we felt when we came back and won in 2014 was incredible. If we had won the title in 2013, maybe we wouldn't have won it in 2014. That disappointment surely made us a little stronger. It revealed the team's true character. Losing this way in 2013, and then beating the same team in the Finals the following year, shows mental strength.

The Peak

In 2014, when we knew we were going to play against Miami again in the Finals, losing became an impossibility. Tim and I talked about nothing else. We were not going to lose twice in a row to the same team. It was *impossible*. Besides, we played so well the whole year. We never, not once, talked about revenge. We wanted to be NBA champions, plain and simple. The images from the 2013 Finals did not taint the 2014 Finals. The only time that Pop showed them to us was at the beginning of the season, on the very first day of practice.

We got to the arena, happy to see each other and to kick off a new season, only to be told we didn't have practice. Instead, we had to watch the entire fourth quarter and the overtime of that Game 6. It hurt, and it reminded us of a big loss, but it was a good way to start the season and motivate us. For me, it was all the harder to return, as I had just come back all pumped over my European championship title. I had a wicked amount of energy. "It's on again. Let's go!" And—bam! Pop took us right back down to the bottom of the hole. While enjoying the summer and the huge adventure I'd experienced with the French national team, I had forgotten how much it hurt.

In 2014, we showed another way to win an NBA title with a passing game that had rarely been seen in the NBA since the days of Magic Johnson and Larry Bird. Between 2012 and 2014, that was kind of our peak. Our game was praised by the entire NBA, and everyone loved watching us play. It was a European kind of game. A passing game. A game made for me.

Not to brag, but 2014 was maybe one of the best years for basketball in the history of the sport. You could compare us to the Lakers and the Celtics in the 1980s. That year, we reached an incredible level. For me, it was the best basketball I'd played with the Spurs.

Our performance in the Finals was impressive. Miami decided to trap me with two players. Once I got rid of the ball, Boris Diaw and Kawhi Leonard were the ones who had to create a play for us. I knew that Boris, with that play in particular, was really great. He was like the Spurs' second point guard. Boris had a magnificent series. In Games 3 and 4, Kawhi was incredible offensively. He also played incredible defense against LeBron James. In Game 5, we won by 20 points, and that was the high point.

Winning an NBA title with my childhood friend was an incredible feeling. Boris and I would sometimes talk about it at INSEP and laughed about it. We had never really dreamed of it coming true. That both of us could one day play in the NBA was already crazy. That we could then play on the same team was even crazier. But then when we won an NBA title together, it was completely impossible to have dreamed of that.

When he got to San Antonio in the 2011–12 season, we were happy to see each other again. Boris stayed at my guest house for two months. In general, people take two weeks to find a house. Bobo was so comfortable at my house that he stayed for two months. I was happy to have him. Boris is like family. He is really respectful. He always asked me if he could come to the house, or if he could eat with us in the evening. We had great times together, and it was the first time since INSEP that we saw each other so much through the year. It was different from the French national team. They were special times. We would eat dinner together. We talked about everything, and not just basketball. We obviously also talked about the Spurs, and I helped him with the integration process. Now, when I reflect back on it, it wasn't only the 2014 NBA title, but also the 2013 European championship title, which we both took back to San Antonio. Winning two major titles with your childhood friend is really wild.

The 2014 season created an incredible amount of enthusiasm around Boris and me. All of our friends were there. There were a lot of French people. It was really nice. We celebrated that together for a long time.

For me, 2014 was a crazy year. We were NBA champions in mid-June, and Josh, my first child, was born a little before, in April. In the final days of Axelle's pregnancy, I made nonstop trips between the hospital and the gym, even though we were in the middle of the playoffs. I wasn't sleeping a lot, but I sure had good games on the court. Then, in the wake of all that, that summer, on August 2, Axelle and I got married. It was an incredible year for me. It was so emotionally rich. I admit that after, I was a little worn down. Boris was brave enough to go on to the World Cup with the French national team. I decided to take a summer off. I was beat.

The 2014 title undoubtedly means the most to me. It's also the one that really made me conscious of all the sacrifices that were necessary to win an NBA title. That year I felt like everything was in slow motion. I was able to appreciate each moment. In 2003, I hadn't made many memories because everything was moving so fast in my mind, but I remember every moment from 2014.

Before Game 5, a home game, I rented a 60-seat bus for all of my friends to attend the game. It was a party bus with music, strobe lights, everything. We were confident. We were leading the series 3–1, and we needed to finish the job. Nothing was final yet, but like I said, it was impossible for us to lose.

At the end of the game, I didn't leave with the team. I left in the bus to go to the restaurant and took the trophy along with me. All of my friends were able to get their picture taken with the trophy. I went home at dawn in the bus, and still I kept the trophy. I was able to get a picture of it with Josh. In the morning, Tom James, the Spurs' director of communication, called me. He was a little panicked and was looking for the trophy.

"Tony, where is the trophy? Do you have it?"

No one remembered anything. Everyone was drunk, and no one could even remember that I had taken it. I had to take it back to the club quickly that morning because it was supposed to be the official picture day.

What I experienced in San Antonio fulfilled me beyond all my childhood dreams. Going somewhere else, to another market or another NBA franchise, never crossed my mind until I left for Charlotte in my last year. I was happy in San Antonio. We were winning, and I wasn't worried. I never played basketball for the money. I didn't mind making less and having my career there. Tim, Manu, and I always took less money to stay in San Antonio and have a good team around us. The glory, New York, Los Angeles—none of it interested me much. In San Antonio, the fans and team adopted me, and it was logical for me to stay there. I could have easily earned $30 or $40 million more in my career if I had gone elsewhere. But I was happy, and that was worth all the money in the world, even if Pop occasionally drove me nuts.

Sometimes the assistant coach would tell me, "I know you're annoyed with Pop tonight. If you wake up tomorrow and you're still annoyed, that means there's a problem. If you've forgotten about it when you wake up, that means it's all good."

Well, every morning, when I woke up, I had already forgotten about it. I'm not one to hold a grudge. I don't forget, which is different. Whenever I didn't agree, I would wake up in the morning, eat breakfast, and hit the road. Without being annoyed, I'd go knock on his office door when I got to the training facility to tell him that I didn't agree. Even if it was sometimes hard, I couldn't have imagined a better coach. If I had to do it again, knowing what would happen, I wouldn't change a thing. I would do it all over again. Like he said, I think what he experienced with me also made him a better coach.

My Heart and My Head

I also had the privilege and the chance to rub shoulders with another great coach once in my life: Phil Jackson. It was during the 2009 All-Star Game. It was almost surreal for me. I mean, it was Phil Jackson. He coached Michael Jordan and Kobe Bryant.

It was only an All-Star Game, something festive, but it was interesting to see how he acted with the players, how he talked to them. He had this ability to interact with the players. For me, it was a childhood dream come true: "Wow, I was coached by Phil Jackson!" He was really close to the players and very philosophical. Sometimes we kind of asked ourselves what he was trying to say, but the weekend we spent with him was really awesome.

In my opinion, my best NBA season was in 2013. That's when I felt I was kind of being cheated out of the All-NBA teams. The voting journalists gave the point guard position on the first team to Chris Paul, even though I felt that I really deserved it in 2013. Three years in a row, 2012, 2013, and 2014, I was All-NBA second team. They could have given me a spot on the first team at least once out of the three. During that time, I could almost say that I was the best point guard in the NBA. But in 2013, I believe I was the best point guard in the world. I'm not being conceited—everyone was saying it.

I was disappointed, of course, to never have been named to the All-NBA First Team. But I don't regret it. For me, Popovich was the most important judge of my game. I was the best point guard in the NBA in his eyes. So as long as Pop and Duncan saw me like that, I was fine with it.

I'll never forget the day the results were released in 2013. We were in the conference finals, and it was after Game 2 against Memphis. That night I scored 15 points, with 18 assists. It was my personal record for assists in one NBA game.

The results came out. Tim was first team. I was second. He came to see me, looking a little sorry, his head lowered.

"If we're here today, Tony, it's because you played like a candidate for the MVP award the entire season. In my opinion, you're the best point guard in the NBA, and you deserve being first team a lot more than me because you're the leader that carries our team today."

Those words truly touched me. They were worth all of the recognition and rankings in the world. The fact that Duncan—the best power forward in the history of the NBA, the one who hadn't even spoken to me during my whole first year, and who thought that we could never win a title with that little European point guard—told me that was worth more than anything. I cared more about Duncan and Popovich appreciating and respecting me than I did the journalists, who were clearly more numerous in Los Angeles (at the time Chris Paul was playing for the Clippers) than in San Antonio.

From 2012 to 2014, we made it to the NBA Finals twice and won an NBA title. I know that I'm French, but still.

I'm not taking anything away from Chris Paul. He's an incredible point guard and a friend of mine too. He'd say he was the best, and I'd say I was the best. That's normal—we were rivals. But over the course of three years, he didn't even make it to the conference finals.

At any rate, I never could have imagined being the best point guard in the world at any stage of my career. It's actually kind of wild. Technically, there was nothing I truly excelled at. The three-point shot? No. Dribbling? No—I'm not like Kyrie Irving. The only thing that you could give me first place for, along with Allen Iverson, was speed. I had to work on everything else.

But there are two things you can't take away from me: my heart and my head. My determination. That's what has made the difference, I think. It's true that when you look at my physique compared to the standards for an NBA player, I don't look like much. A little bit like Tom Brady, and yet, he did crazy things with his head and arm. For me, it was my head and my speed. One day, Isiah Thomas said in *L'Équipe* magazine that I was the Tom Brady of my sport. It's a nice statement.

All this takes me way back. When I got to the NBA, I knew what the Americans thought of European shooting guards and point guards. They couldn't play in the NBA, etc. I took it as my obligation to change this opinion, telling myself that if I didn't make it, they would continue to say it. I took it as a challenge to carry the reputation of all the European point guards.

I was familiar with Drazen Petrovic's story. He was the first European to succeed in the NBA as a shooting guard. He had been an All-Star in 1993 and was rising quickly to the top when, unfortunately, he was killed in a car accident. He was an inspiration for European shooting guards. He was the first to have succeeded.

On the other end, a legendary point guard in Europe, Sasha Djordjevic, hadn't succeeded in the NBA. But I knew that my game would be better suited to the NBA than his. I didn't tell myself, "Djordjevic didn't make it. Rigadeau didn't really succeed. Mous Sonko (who had had a tryout in Vancouver in 2000) didn't either. Just like all those who came before me, it's going to be hard for me too." My game was different from their games. It was unique. A lot of coaches pointed it out. I told myself that I could make it in the NBA because of my speed.

San Antonio was the ideal franchise for my game. Even though I like creativity and speed, I also like a game to be structured. I like knowing where my teammates are when I get in, so that it's not a free-for-all. I never dreamed about a club where I could do what I want or take 30 shots. What would have been the point? I quickly realized that sharing with Tim and Manu, scoring 18-20 points per game, and having a chance to win the title was a lot more interesting than scoring 27 or 28 points and being eliminated during the first round of the playoffs. For example, Russell Westbrook's career didn't interest me. It's not what I wanted to do.

Today I reflect on all these records we broke with the Spurs. I was so young when I got there. In terms of precociousness for point and shooting guard positions, you can only compare me to Magic Johnson and Kobe Bryant.

Regarding the number of titles, points, and assists before the age of 25, only Kobe and Magic have records like mine.

Once you're in the NBA, and your dream has come true, and you also have been lucky enough to win a title very early on, you have to find other goals to keep you focused. For me, my motivation was making history in my sport. With the Spurs, I knew that I had huge opportunities to achieve that. I don't have benchmark games or memories that strike me. My best NBA moments are my four titles. I don't have an emotion or something in particular that stayed with me. Often, during the season, you kind of live like a robot. In the end, there aren't really a lot of emotions. You do your job. You know where you want to go, and you know it's going to be a long trip. It's only when you win a title that you really let your emotions come out.

If I had to think of a few cherished moments, one would obviously be the day I was drafted. The day I heard my name and saw myself walk up to the platform to shake hands with David Stern, the NBA commissioner. Of course that's a day that means more than others. There are also games that have stuck with me more than others. Game 6 in the conference finals against Dallas in 2003 comes to mind, when Steve Kerr was on fire, and we reached my first NBA Finals. Game 3 of those same Finals, when I dominated Jason Kidd. I scored 26 points that night, and I felt like I was at the top of the NBA. Game 5 in the conference semifinals against Phoenix in 2007 was huge, because we knew that if we won that series, we would be champions.

Still, the biggest, most important moments are the titles. That's where everything came together, and I felt like I had completed my mission. Those emotions are difficult to explain. Each season has its own story, its own identity, its own images.

I remember when Michael Finley joined the Spurs in 2006. That season, we lost the playoffs against Dallas in Game 7. In the locker room, he had tears in his eyes and that really made me sad. I had already won two titles. He had never won one and had come to San Antonio for that purpose. So the following season, 2006–07, I wanted to win a title for him. I wanted to see him happy and to be able to tell him, "You made a good decision coming here. You won the title."

In 2003, when I won the title, I knew that I wasn't yet the player I wanted to become. I had won a title. That was huge. Duncan had carried us, but I could still get better. You need two things for a career to be complete: collective success and individual fulfillment. To win other titles with Duncan, I knew that Manu and I had to become stars.

Changing Perceptions

When I got to San Antonio, I was so young that the fans kind of looked at me like their son. They took to me very quickly, and I immediately felt a lot of love. It surprised me. I had played in Paris. There wasn't an audience, and I had never felt a crowd that loves you and is behind you, and lives for the team's results.

Today, I have forged 15 years of relationships with fans and entrepreneurs who were in the stadium. For a few years, I held poker tournaments and a decent number of fans came to play at my house. We are the city's only pro sport, so wherever we go, there are Spurs fans. There's a special bond between the Spurs and the city of San Antonio. It was nothing like that in Charlotte, where I played my final NBA season.

Along with fellow European players Dirk Nowitzki and Pau Gasol, I think we broke boundaries. After us, the Americans' mentality changed, and all the teams wanted Europeans on board: the future Dirks, Paus, and Tonys. It really took off at an incredible rate.

I remember Nikoloz Tskitishvili, who was picked fifth in the 2002 draft. Why? You can't say he was the best. But everyone wanted a European. It had become trendy. Today, there are over 80 international players in the NBA from the world over. So you bet I'm a little proud to have participated in that change. With Dirk and Pau, we managed to shake things up. Today, it's no longer a huge risk to take on a European point guard. You have Goran Dragić, Luka

Dončić, Ricky Rubio, José Calderón, and others. In my day, it was a crazy bet. It wasn't normal. There wasn't a single one.

My Terrible Injury

I've often talked about how blessed I've been throughout my entire career. Still, I couldn't dodge an injury forever.

It happened on May 2, 2017. We hosted Houston in the conference semifinals for the second game of the series. I was in full swing at the time. I was having a great playoff. I was in touch with my feelings, and Pop even announced plays for me for those playoffs! It was going really well.

We were in the final quarter. I went to make my teardrop, a shot I'd done 50,000 times before, and while jumping in the air, I felt something. When I landed, I knew I was hurt, which is why I missed the teardrop. I dropped the ball, looked at my leg, and felt something. Upon touching the ground, I still didn't realize how serious it was. I said to myself, "That's weird. Did I sprain my knee? Pull a muscle? If I pulled a muscle, I'll be out for three weeks and won't be in shape for the conference finals."

I quickly realized that I couldn't move my leg. Yet I still wasn't worried. Since my knee didn't hurt, I knew it wasn't a cruciate ligament. So I thought it was okay. In my opinion, the cruciates and the Achilles tendon are the two most serious injuries a player can have in basketball. It was only when two of my teammates picked me up off the ground and I leaned on their shoulders that I realized how bad it was. I still couldn't walk. They carried me to the sideline, and then I was taken to the locker room in a wheelchair and placed onto the physical therapist's table.

When the doctor looked at my leg, he saw that it was hollow, as if there was a hole beneath the skin, just above the knee. My tendon had snapped and was all the way up my thigh. I had nothing holding my leg in place. Nothing that would let me stand up or let me walk. I couldn't even bend my leg a few millimeters. I was paralyzed. I saw on the doctor's face that it was serious.

"What is it, Doc?"

"You no longer have a tendon!"

"So what is it?"

"I think you ruptured your tendon in the left quad."

"How long will it take? A month?"

"You don't understand, Tony. That's what holds up your entire leg. It's worse than the Achilles tendon! It will take 10 months."

I started to cry. I didn't know what to say. I understood without really comprehending. He warned me right away that I had to prepare myself for a long rehabilitation.

"You're going to be paralyzed for three weeks. You cannot move your leg at all."

"So it will take a long time, but I'll come back regardless, right?"

"I'm not sure."

Right there, I didn't believe him. In my mind, I was going to come back. It was impossible to believe otherwise. It was impossible that this would end my career. Impossible for me to never play again. I asked him if I had to have surgery.

"Of course—you don't have a tendon anymore. You have to have surgery within 48 hours. It's a complete break. You have 24 hours to see if you want to do the surgery with us or get a second opinion."

I replied, "I've been here for 17 years. I'm doing this with you. I trust you. If you're able to perform this kind of surgery, then let's do it. I don't need to talk to anyone else."

Everyone was shocked at the time. I had never been hurt throughout my entire career. No one was used to seeing me in that state. And no one really understood my injury. What's a ruptured tendon in the quadriceps?

Pop was on the verge of tears. He hugged me closely: "I'm so sorry. I'm so sorry. It's my fault." He felt he could have taken me out or had me not play as much. I reassured him: "No one could have predicted this, and you had me rest throughout the entire regular season. It's not your fault. It's part of the game. That's just how it is."

Five minutes after the diagnosis in the locker room, I switched gears. I needed to be positive. Half the battle with rehab is in your mind. I was going to come back. It would take a while. I would have to be patient, but I couldn't go out this way.

We left the stadium very late. Axelle brought the car. On the ride home, she was sad for me, and I could feel her anxiety. When you don't know exactly how severe your injury is, you ask yourself the most basic questions. Will I walk normally again? Will I limp? Will I be able to play sports again one day? We were all having those kinds of doubts.

The next day I had an MRI to verify the diagnosis. The doctor was sure, though I was still hoping that he was wrong. But no matter how much I told myself that, I still couldn't move my leg at all. Axelle helped me carry my leg so I could go to the bathroom. I could do nothing alone. That lasted another three weeks.

Eventually, I had surgery. It took an hour. My tendon was reattached. I left the hospital straight afterward. Axelle took me back home in a boot and a huge splint that covered my entire leg. "Titi" Henry came to spend a few days in San Antonio just to make sure I was doing well and to offer his support. That night, he was the one who helped me go to the bathroom.

I was optimistic when I learned that the surgery went really well. But there was no doubt about it—the road ahead was going to be very long. I was going to have to be patient and stick to the instructions.

The longest part of the entire process was the first three weeks. I couldn't move my leg at all. During the first few weeks, I just needed to be able to move it a few more degrees and to be able to lift my leg a few inches. I still had the staples and bandages for the first 10 days. My leg had been so swollen that I couldn't do anything. After 10 days, the staples were removed. Okay, first battle won!

My first big achievement was when I could move my leg about a third of an inch, and not much more. I had used all my strength to do it, but it made me so happy I had tears in my eyes. My leg was coming back to life and moving again. It had taken me three weeks. Ten days prior, no matter how hard I focused like a madman to try to move my leg, it wouldn't budge. I was frustrated: "Why won't it move?" The physical therapist reassured me and said not to worry and keep trying. So I kept trying. But if you've never had an injury, and you want to lift your leg less than an inch and you can't do it, it's difficult to understand.

Those close to me were very worried. When you're used to seeing your brother, your friend, your husband be Superman or a war machine, and suddenly he can't do anything by himself, it's very strange. I reassured them: "We'll bounce back."

A Long Round of Rehabilitation

The whole long process was a series of small victories.

I stayed in San Antonio for the first three months before going back to France. The rehab sessions started after four weeks, but I couldn't really do much. In the beginning, I would try every day to bend my leg a few inches. But it locked up quickly. Progress was minimal at first. I did that exercise for 20 minutes, three times a day. The rest of the time I had to rest. After six weeks, I could finally put my foot on the ground. One day, at ASVEL, Yoann Casin, the French national team's physical therapist, told me, "Tony, it's going to be hard. It's going to take a long time! Don't worry. It'll come back."

I had scheduled my vacation, two weeks on a boat, like I did every summer. I told the Spurs that I couldn't cancel it. I had already paid. So the club's staff sent someone who would be on the boat with me every day. That's how Marylin came with us on the boat for two weeks. It was a free vacation. She was so happy. We went to Saint-Tropez, Corsica, and Monte Carlo. She had never been on a private yacht, with a personal chef cooking all your meals. She was delighted.

I could only "work" on the boat in the morning. The rest of the day, my leg had to rest. It was about four months after the operation, so of course I still couldn't run or jump. But I could move around, and at least walk calmly. Every morning I would wake up at 7:00 AM. Marilyn and I would go walk around for an hour, sometimes two. We got off the boat and walked in town, but only on paths that weren't too steep. It was early, silent, and peaceful. I remember a walk in Corsica, near Bonifacio. We stayed there for two days. The scenery and the cliffs in the early morning were magnificent. We took long walks to get my mind used to moving my leg and building up muscle again. I had never walked so much in my life as I did during that time.

When it comes down to it, I didn't really like it. But I got used to it. Today I still like waking up early and going for a walk around my neighborhood. I've learned to appreciate those moments of calm and silence, and the pleasure of discovering nature as it wakes up. Before my injury that would never have happened. Despite the injury, it was nice to take a little time and talk about life. My life had always been on the fast track. Then, suddenly, there was no risk of my going very fast. I had plenty of time.

The hardest thing for me was the stairs. Something that would have taken me two minutes under normal circumstances took me 20 minutes. One day, in Saint-

Tropez, I wasn't able to climb the stairs to the top of the city by myself to see the view. Just lifting my leg to reach the next step took a superhuman amount of effort. I was drenched in sweat, which seemed insane. But going back down was even worse. Simply bending my leg made my entire body shake. That day, seeing how hard it was to walk down a stairway, I realized that I had a long road ahead of me to be able to play basketball again.

After those morning walks, we would go back to the boat, and I would do a little weightlifting. They were simple things, with small weights. I worked on bending. I worked on strengthening my ankle and so on. Then Marylin would give me a small medical treatment. She worked on my scar for at least 45 minutes to soften the area that had been operated on. It was laborious for her every day. Then there was a massage, stretching, and after lunch I was free. But I couldn't really do much. When my friends left to go jet-skiing, I wasn't allowed. Still, it was really nice to be able to do my rehab under such conditions and in the middle of such beautiful scenery. It puts you in a positive state of mind. It wasn't the end of the world. The injury really made me look at things differently. It allowed me to appreciate the simple things in life even more.

Today my leg is no longer like it was before the injury, and it never will be again. Extending my left leg takes more effort than it does with my right one. When I wake up in the morning, I can feel it's not as strong. I'll have to strengthen it and stay active for the rest of my life, because it kind of hurts otherwise. I have some complications, but at least it forces me to train. I'm such a foodie, so exercise is important for my general health. If I think about my injury, I end up telling myself that life has a funny way of working out. It's going to force me to play sports, and so it will stop me from getting too fat.

Rehab on the Great Wall of China

About two weeks after vacation, I went to China. I had obligations to fulfill regarding my partnerships, and I didn't want to cancel. I was starting to jog a bit and climb stairs a bit faster. I went to the Great Wall to practice climbing the stairs.

I started to see the light at the end of the tunnel in China. I could walk without limping. The hardest part was getting my mind used to those movements again. Once it gives your body and leg the right information, you know you're getting somewhere. It took a long time to come back. For three weeks before my vacation, I did sessions with little electrodes on my head to stimulate that connection. In China, I was five months post-op. It wasn't too bad. I knew it was only a matter of time before I could run or sidestep again. Just a matter of time before I could finally play basketball again.

When I got back to San Antonio, the physiotherapy work changed, and the Spurs' physical trainer took over. Every day I did weightlifting but couldn't play basketball. The workload wasn't too heavy. It was just continuity to get my body used to it again. I also did stretches to regain flexibility.

During that period, the hardest thing for me was to watch what I was eating. It was summertime and vacation. Early on, since I couldn't move at all, I really had to watch what I ate. It wasn't easy. But I was serious and determined. I really wanted to come back, and I knew that eating well was crucial. "You can do everything right during rehab, but if you eat a lot it won't be good," I told myself. I didn't want food to ruin all the work I was doing.

During training camp at the end of September, I did nothing, but I was there, and I watched. It was pure pleasure to be with my teammates, to share a drill and just be with the group.

I started practicing again seven months after the injury. I felt okay, but I needed to work on my physical conditioning, rhythm, endurance, and cardio. Each day, I felt I was getting better and better. Feeling like you've found yourself is a tremendous feeling. Just dribbling and shooting was pure happiness. But I had to get used to everything again.

In the beginning, each movement was hard. I was also apprehensive during the first week. You don't know how you're going to handle each new movement, each new situation. After a week, I told myself that I couldn't control the injury. If I was going to injure myself again, well, then I would injure myself again. Once you're in that state of mind, afterward it's game on, and pretty quickly.

Everyone on the team was happy to see me again and couldn't wait for me to come back. I missed the first 20 games of the season. During my first home game against Dallas, on November 27, 2017, Popovich immediately put me back in the starting lineup, as if things had returned to normal. The audience gave me a magnificent welcome back. It was kind of like nothing had changed. I was back in business.

It was a great night. That moment was an ultimate victory for me. I managed to overcome the ordeal. I didn't want my career to end because of an injury. Once again, I wasn't overcome with emotion. I was just happy. During the game, I wasn't cautious or apprehensive. I played normally. I wasn't playing at 100 percent, but I felt good. I had made it back.

At the same time, I knew very well that my leg was no longer like it had been before and would never be the same as before. I knew that I couldn't play like I once had, and above all, I could no longer play in back-to-backs because my leg needed a lot of rest. I had the time to get used to the idea. I could only handle a minimum amount of stress.

Pop suspected as much. Regardless of my injury, I was getting older. He was preparing himself for my retirement by having young point guards come out. He had to create a plan for my succession.

Coming Back Slowly

When I got back on the court, I played, but I still wasn't myself. I knew it. The doctor had warned me, "You'll only fully come back next year." The Spurs were always focused on winning championships, and I knew that I wasn't up to par yet. I was actually far from it.

But I was okay with that. I knew I needed time. I could barely walk four months earlier. I didn't put any pressure on myself. I had already won everything during my career, and my body had taken a hit. I needed to accept that. It was certainly the result of everything I had given before. All of those seasons and the summers when I didn't rest much. My body gave out at the end.

When Pop came to see me after about 20 games to explain that, being almost 36 years old, it might be better for me to come off the bench, as Manu did before me, I understood the time had come to make the transition. I was aware of it. I knew I was no longer myself. I took it well, and I knew that it was time.

At some point, you shouldn't lie to yourself. When you're no longer the same player, you know it. And I was no longer the same player, that's all. For me, coming off the bench was a normal transition. The logical continuation. Also, it took pressure off of me. I could easily get back to a respectable level.

I ended the season like that, with the goal of working on my leg all summer, getting stronger, and coming back at 100 percent the following season. I knew that I couldn't do back-to-back games, but I knew that I could play at a good level. Better than what I was then.

Still, I could tell that Pop was hesitant: "We absolutely want to keep you. We want you to finish your career in San Antonio, but you're going to be 37, and we'd prefer it if you were the third point guard, kind of the veteran, and that you take the younger ones under your wing."

It was early July of 2018. I was in France, and Pop explained all of that on the phone. It was the beginning of free agent negotiations, and I was part of it.

I answered, "No, I want to be second point guard. The doctor told me that I'm getting better. Being a veteran, taking younger players under my wing, I would do that naturally. But to never play, honestly, Pop, I can't do that. I can't go out like that. Being third point guard is a *no*. If Charlotte makes me an offer, I won't come back to see if you want to match it. If they make an offer, I'm taking it, and I'm leaving."

Before signing on with Charlotte, I asked Axelle: "If you really want me to stay in San Antonio, I'll do it. I'll do it for our relationship and our family. I'll bite the bullet. I'll be third point guard and stay on the bench. But I'll be here with you. I'm here for you, for the kids. If you really want me to stay, I'll stay."

I had won everything during my career. I had nothing left to prove. Even if I had wanted that last year of playing, it couldn't come before our family. But Axelle said, "No. Go to Charlotte. I'll take care of the family. I want you to finish in a way that's best for you. Have fun. Have a great season. Make the sacrifices worth it and do it well."

Axelle's support was the key element. I could say, "Okay, I'm going!"

Of course, I hesitated before getting her approval. Staying in San Antonio and playing my entire career for one team meant something to me. It was worth it, even if I wasn't going to play during my last year. It was still a beautiful and rare thing. Besides, just one year without playing wasn't going to change my legacy, as Americans like to say.

Pop asked me if I was sure of my decision, and I said, "Yes. I don't want that role." Pop didn't want to change his mind, and I decided to leave. I didn't even care about the $4 million he offered. I think they would have even made the effort to match Charlotte's offer of $5 million. But I didn't want that role. I didn't want to be on the bench for every game and not play. I wanted to show that there was still some gas left in the tank, that I was still able to contribute something.

Actually, I don't really know, and will probably never know, if Pop really thought that I was going to leave. I think that Pop and RC Buford, the general manager, didn't really believe it. Then Charlotte made an offer, and I left. Pop was a little sad, but he understood.

I'm not going to lie. It was a difficult experience. I had really wanted to finish with the Spurs and play my entire career with that club. It was something rare and beautiful in my opinion. But I know it's a business. Like I often say, everything happens for a reason, and I was destined to finish my career in Charlotte.

It was Pop who told me on the phone that the Spurs wouldn't top Charlotte's offer. When you're the head of a club, sometimes you have to make difficult decisions. But I could put myself in his shoes. I'm the head of a club now, and I know what it's like. He told me he would still love me and that I was a Spurs legend.

When I hung up the phone, it felt really weird. I wondered whether I really had done it. But that's life. I told myself that it would be nice to play in Charlotte with Nicolas Batum. We were going to play together and strengthen our business ties for ASVEL.

But there was also Michael Jordan and "Coach JB," James Borrego. JB knew how it was with the Spurs. He was going to take good care of me.

The Lap of Honor in Charlotte

I was so excited to tackle that last season in Charlotte. It was the beginning of a new adventure, and I wanted to have a great season.

It was a radical lifestyle change. I got an apartment in the city center so that I could be close to the gym. If I was going to sacrifice seeing my family for seven or eight months, I might as well make the most of it on the court and take things seriously. I think I managed to do what I had wanted to do during that last year of my career.

However, it was still a shock in the beginning, especially when you get there and you don't know where the gym is, or the locker room, or where your spot in the locker room is. There were only young players on the team. It was completely different than the Spurs. It was not a team of veteran players. Topics of conversation were different. Everything was different. But I adapted quickly. I'm very social and spoke to everyone. I meshed with everyone very quickly and was part of a super group. The players were all nice and wanted to learn. I came from the Spurs, so they all looked at me with respect. They asked a lot of questions.

In August, I stopped the first group practice with them after five minutes. They weren't disciplined at all, and they were kind of all over the place. I got them together and said, "Guys, if we play like that we definitely won't go to the playoffs. We're not going to win a lot of games playing this way. In order to be a good team, you need to develop good habits right away."

I took on the team's leadership. JB was happy. I think that I helped him a lot during his first year as head coach. It wasn't easy for him.

I signed a "one-and-one" contract because I knew from the start that I wasn't sure I'd do a second season. If I'm being completely honest, the moment I signed, I already knew it was more likely that I wouldn't do a second season. I knew it would be hard for my family. I told myself, "I'll do a year and see how it goes." But I think I already knew I wouldn't do a second year.

Looking back, the fact that the first year was athletically complicated and that we didn't make it to the playoffs clearly didn't help. I had always played basketball to win titles.

Each new year with the Spurs, I felt we had a chance to win the title. With Charlotte in 2018, it was the first time I started a season knowing we had zero chance to win. Given the team, making the playoffs would already be a hell of an accomplishment. But we didn't make it.

Then again, when I weighed everything, my family's and children's happiness was more important to me than the $7 or $8 million I could have earned by playing a second season in Charlotte. When I made the decision, I knew that my advisers would want me to do that last year, because I had contracts with sponsors that would only happen if I played. But I went against their opinion. I was happy this way, and I did what I had to do.

I wouldn't change anything in my career—nothing at all. If I felt like that, it meant I could retire. I was peaceful and happy. So why spend one more year far away from my family? It was pointless. Besides, it was physically hard for me. It was getting harder and harder. I didn't want to play a season where I wouldn't be happy or where I might hurt myself. Can you imagine injuring an Achilles tendon or a knee? That's a horrible end. Physically, I felt I'd come to the end.

Returning to San Antonio as a Hornet

The thing that comforted me in my decision to only do one year in Charlotte was returning to San Antonio on January

15, 2019. We had come to play the Spurs, and I was wearing a Hornets jersey.

I received an incredible welcome from the Spurs fans that overwhelmed me and reminded me that my NBA career was there, and nowhere else. From that moment on, I knew I wouldn't do a second year.

That night after the game, I had a long discussion with Axelle. It had been seven months since I'd left. The game in San Antonio had made me very nostalgic. Not long after, during the All-Star Game break in February, I spent a week at my house, without basketball, and it went great. I told myself I liked my life like that too. And then doubt disappeared.

Closing the book on a season with Michael Jordan as the big boss isn't insignificant, either. The circle was complete. He was my idol, the one who was plastered all over my childhood bedroom walls and who had inspired me. Even if he hadn't been around much during that season, he had been there for a few practices. He had made a couple of shots and sat in on one or two film sessions with us. He was real. He still loved talking about basketball. Sometimes we would text each other after the games. I was the veteran. He would occasionally come to me to take the team's pulse.

I was pleased with this last adventure. I had a better season than the year before. You could call it a mini comeback. We had a couple of quality wins, and I had some throwback, old-school games. When I scored more than 20 points in a game, I told myself that the wine I had drunk the night before must have been good because I didn't hurt anywhere.

Each time I finished a throwback game, Pop and RC Buford would call me. The Spurs coaches texted me. They followed me, supported me throughout the season. When I scored 24 points against Miami in the seventh game of the season, Pop called me laughing, "Oh! No kidding!" I set a few more all-time records. I gained a few more "best scorer" and "best passer" rankings. It was a really nice season.

Even at the End, I Was There

I have no regrets for having ended my career that way, without having played the last month of the regular season. None. We weren't going to qualify for the playoffs. In mid-March, there were 12 games left, and we were behind by five wins. We were definitely lucky. Suddenly, our young players beat Boston despite us being behind by 18 points in the fourth quarter. There was Jeremy Lamb's miraculous winning shot in Toronto. We couldn't have predicted all of that.

In the end, in the last few games, we still had a chance, but fate still wasn't on our side. And it wasn't even my decision.

In mid-March, one month from the end of the regular season, the coach said to me, "TP, we really only have a slim chance at the playoffs, and I know that you won't really be motivated to play under those conditions. I want to put the young players in. What do you think?"

"Yeah, that's a good idea, but I'm coming back if we make it to the playoffs, okay?"

That was the deal. We were really low in the standings, and he wanted to put the young players in. I respected that. Then a dynamic was set in motion. The younger players were playing well, so you stick with it.

As for me, I stayed in shape throughout that time and continued to practice. Honestly, since we didn't qualify for the playoffs, I didn't care about ending my career like that, one month before the end of the regular season. I had shown throughout the season that I was there.

Very early on in my career, I had wanted to make history in my sport. That's what had motivated me. Asserting that very early had given me a goal and carried me for a long time. It's so hard for athletes to stay motivated once they become champions and reach the top. I think the endurance at the height of my career will be the hardest thing to attain for the next great French basketball player. I hope there will be another French NBA champion and All-Star. I hope so for French basketball. But it's going to be hard to catch up with my endurance. Playing 20 pro seasons, winning four NBA titles, and staying at the top for so long is no easy feat.

People are going to realize I'm no longer there, and they'll watch the young players, the Evan Fourniers and Rudy Goberts. They'll watch their playoff games. They're going to understand how hard it is to play in the playoffs.

At one point, the fans almost thought it was easy to score 20 points in a playoff game, or win a series, or be the MVP in the Finals. "He's Tony Parker. It's normal for him to do that." But it's really hard. I'm among the top 10 scorers and passers in NBA playoff history. It's a huge source of pride for me. But I don't think there will be many French players who will make it to the Hall of Fame.

Retiring didn't upset me all that much. I'm not even sure I'll miss it. My leg will never be the same, I'll never be the old Tony Parker again, so I wasn't interested in continuing. Playing for fun? No problem. I'll play. I'm passionate about it. But I won't miss the competition and the NBA.

I will always be nostalgic when thinking back on the years with the Spurs. Tim and I talk about it a lot. We know that nothing will ever be the same. But we can't do anything about it. Now we just need to enjoy our lives and everything we've accomplished.

I'm happy and at peace in my house in San Antonio, finally able to spend time with all the people I was never able to see. Between the preseason, the regular season, and the French national team in the summer, everything went by so fast. I can't wait to start doing the things I always wanted to do: skiing, traveling, going on a safari, going to the Australian Open. I have a lot of things I want to do that I never had time for. For the past 18 years, I haven't been to France from late September to early May or June. I just want to spend a winter there. It's a small thing, but it's been such a long time since I've been able to do it.

Of course, I'm going to follow the NBA. One of my dreams is to one day be part of an NBA club. It's a distant dream. But you need to have dreams. Being a minority stakeholder in an NBA franchise sounds good. Owner, not so much. It's impossible today given how much franchises are worth. But I would be fine with having one foot in. I've put down the ball, but I haven't given up on the sport.

When my sons, Josh and Liam, are old enough to want to know what I did with the first part of my life, I'll tell them to read this book. When they're older, and a little better able to understand, I'll be able to talk to them about my career. For now, I'm letting them grow up and enjoy their childhood. Josh is more into baseball for now and for Liam, it's the piano.

MY PHOTOS

Like any child, I first found comfort in the arms of my mother, Pamela. Very quickly, I started following my dad to his basketball practices. I was barely three years old and my first ball was almost bigger than me!

Even though I was young myself, I always took great care of my younger brother, TJ. A protective hand on his shoulder, and a ball on my knee, of course!

My entire family: my father, TP Senior; my mother, Pamela; and my brothers, TJ and Pierre. Despite the divorce of my parents, I have always felt their presence. They have always been there for me.

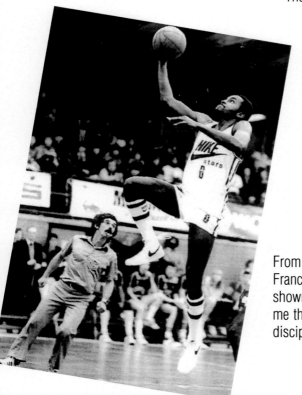

From the Netherlands to France, my father has always shown the way. He instilled in me the American mentality of discipline and self-confidence.

In Dieppe, with my father and my brothers, where we learned to live together. It was difficult for my mother. But she wasn't far; she lived in Fécamp and came to see us during the holidays.

During school holidays, we spent time with our mother. We played tennis and had picnics by the lake with our Saint Bernard. My mother had that bohemian side, where life was a bit of an adventure with her.

Sitting on the side of the road or on a walk in Normandy, we were always with our Saint Bernard and the famous Citroen 2CV that was such a part of my teenage years.

I spent my first two professional seasons in Paris. The first year, in the shadow of Laurent Sciarra, I didn't play much but I learned a lot. Then I became the starting point guard in my second season. (C. Steenkeste / Presse Sports)

At INSEP, with Ronny Turiaf and Boris Diaw. We were inseparable. We were also together at Euro 2003. That year I was team captain of France. Maybe it was a bit early. We finished fourth. That team also had Jérôme Moïso, Florent Pietrus, and Moustapha Sonko.

(Top, Left: N. Luttiau / L'Équipe; Top, Right: F. Carol / Presse Sports; Bottom: C. Ludovic / Presse Sports)

My first time playing for the French team on November 22, 2000, against Turkey.
(P. Lablatiniere / L'Équipe)

After Euro 2001, I arrived in Texas. This was taken outside the Alamodome, the old home of the Spurs.
(C. Steenkeste / Presse Sports)

I didn't expect everything to go so quickly when I reached the NBA. When Gregg Popovich told me that I would be starting my fifth game, I was surprised but I knew I was ready. (C. Steenkeste / Presse Sports)

In France, San Antonio, or New York, Thierry "Titi" Henry is still a friend.
(P. Rondeau / L'Équipe)

In the locker room in 2003, the year of my first NBA title. I was in good company, surrounded by Malik Rose and Bruce Bowen. And the great David Robinson was not far away!

At 21, I am an NBA champion, in just my second season! Everything was going very fast already, but I had only one thing in mind when I lifted this first trophy: win again! (J. Prevost / L'Équipe)

Euro 2005 in Serbia is a painful memory for me. The first week, I didn't play well and even doubted myself a little. Then, there was this cruel defeat in the semifinal against Greece, which deprived us of the title of European champion.
(N. Luttiau / L'Équipe)

A few days before the 2006 World Cup in Japan, I hurt my finger in a game against Brazil. Here beside my father, the competition was already over for me.
(A. Mounic / L'Équipe)

In Houston in 2006, my first All-Star Game. Steve Nash (opposite), Kobe Bryant, Tracy McGrady, Kevin Garnett, Yao Ming; I felt like I had joined a family of NBA stars.
(L. Hahn / L'Équipe)

My third NBA title in 2007 is obvioulsy special for me. I was named the Finals MVP, a recognition that no European had ever received before. (Panoramic)

The 2011–12 season was a major turning point in my career. After winning the silver medal at the Euro, Gregg Popovich called me into his office and gave me the keys to the San Antonio Spurs, with full support from Tim Duncan. It was up to me to carry the franchise. (J. Hanish / US PressWire / Presse Sports)

It wasn't always easy, but Gregg Popovich was there for me throughout my career. I know our relationship meant a lot to both of us. (L. Hahn / L'Équipe)

Eventually, it was me who sat in the coach's chair and spoke to the team during timeouts. (L. Hahn / L'Équipe)

Beating Spain in the semifinals of the Euro 2013 is one of the most emotional memories I have from my time wearing the blue jersey. After this victory, I knew that we wouldn't lose in the final against Lithuania. (Expa / Presse Sports)

Euro 2013 was the pinnacle of my career with the French team, after chasing that dream for more than 10 years. (Expa / Presse Sports)

My association with the French national team is a long story, but above all, it's a great love story. I kept coming back to it. I was selected the best player of Euro 2013. Total happiness.

(Expa / Presse Sports)

Winning Euro 2013 and then my fourth NBA crown with the Spurs in 2014 made for an incredible, almost magical year. I fulfilled my mission by leading my teams to the title.
(L. Hahn / L'Équipe)

With Axelle in 2014. Our first child, Josh, was born a few weeks earlier.

In my trophy room at home, jerseys from the four NBA title teams and six All-Star Games have a prominent place. My rings are also carefully preserved. In 18 seasons with the Spurs, I left my imprint in Texas, even on my license plate! (Top: J. Glassberg / L'Équipe; Middle: L. Hahn / L'Équipe)

In 2015, I was 33 years old, and I knew I wasn't as fast as I was at 23. But I knew I could still be a major factor for the Spurs and that I had more good years to come. (USA Today / Presse Sports)

Euro 2015 in France ended well, with a bronze medal. But I was disappointed not to have played at my best in the semifinal against Spain. (R. Martin / L'Équipe)

In 2015, I was 33 years old, and I knew I wasn't as fast as I was at 23. But I knew I could still be a major factor for the Spurs and that I had more good years to come. (USA Today / Presse Sports)

The next generatio
of French players
including Evan Fournie
and Rudy Gobert, wa
ready to take over. M
job was to show ther
the way. (R. Martin / L'Équip

Euro 2015 in France ended well, with a bronze medal. But I was disappointed not to have played at my best in the semifinal against Spain. (R. Martin / L'Équipe)

The 2016–17 season ended in disappointment thanks to my thigh injury during the playoffs. But I got the chance to share the adventure with Pau Gasol, friend and Spanish basketball star.

(Top: Soobum Im; Middle: USA Today / Presse Sports; Bottom: J. Glassberg / L'Équipe)

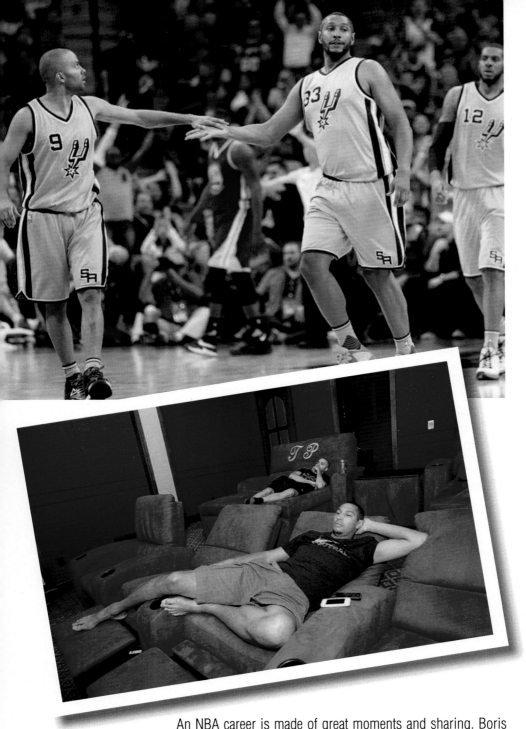

An NBA career is made of great moments and sharing. Boris Diaw, one of my best friends since INSEP, and I never imagined playing in the NBA together. And in 2014, we both won a title!

(Top: E. Schlegel / USA Today Sports / Presse Sports; Bottom: C. Steenkeste / Presse Sports)

Before getting injured in the playoffs against Houston in 2017, I felt that I was gaining speed and was feeling good. (USA Today / Presse Sports)

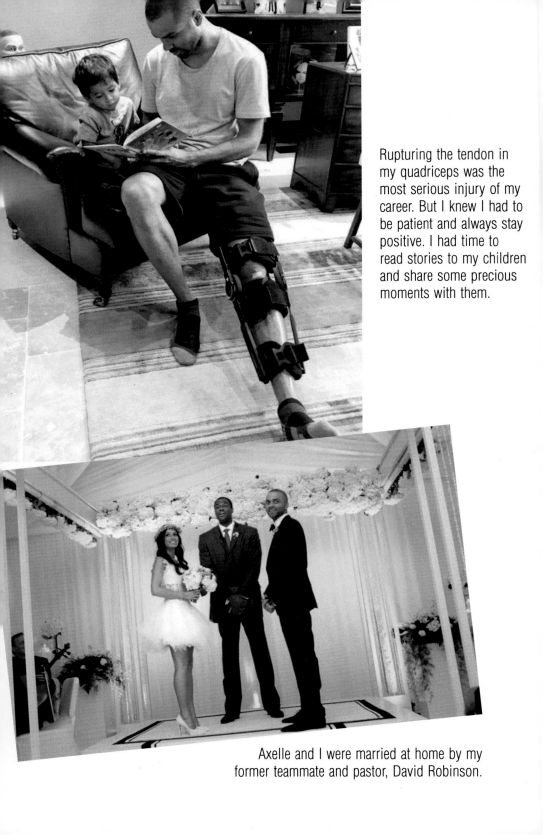

Rupturing the tendon in my quadriceps was the most serious injury of my career. But I knew I had to be patient and always stay positive. I had time to read stories to my children and share some precious moments with them.

Axelle and I were married at home by my former teammate and pastor, David Robinson.

Even though my businesses keep me busy, the family remains my very first priority. Taking a stroll with Josh and Liam. These are the moments in life that are priceless.

Back on the floor seven months after my injury, but I am obviously far from my best. But I returned without apprehension. (USA Today / Presse Sports)

With my friend Nicolas Batum involved at ASVEL, our goal is clear: to make ASVEL a big European club in the years to come. (A. Martin / L'Équipe)

In Charlotte, for my 18th and final season in the NBA. I had come full circle, with Michael Jordan as my boss and Nicolas Batum as my teammate. Even though we missed the playoffs, I was happy with how things turned out. (Top: P. Lahalle / L'Équipe; Bottom: J. Brevard / L'Équipe)

Twelve incredible covers of

L'Équipe featuring yours truly

CHAPTER THREE

My Life in France

My association with the French national team is a long story, but above all, it's a great love story. I kept coming back to it. I was determined. I think my attachment to the team and that jersey can be summed up in one anecdote.

It was the morning of the 2013 EuroBasket finals, and I was in my hotel room. It was a few hours away from game time. I couldn't wait for the game, but I was calm. I was reading the reviews and skimming the newspapers. I was receiving so many texts that I had trouble concentrating on what I was reading. And each time I read one, I could feel my eyes welling up with tears. There were so many expectations and hopes in those messages. It had been so many years— more than 10—that I had been fighting to win with that team. That is when, all of a sudden, I realized just how much it meant to me. I couldn't get a grip on my emotions. That day, in my hotel room, I told myself that it was maybe my last chance to win a title with the French national team. I was reading all of those incoming words, and my feelings just overflowed.

People wanted me to win so badly with the French team. They wrote to me that I deserved it, and that because I was coming back all of those summers, I was going to be rewarded. That morning, in my room, I told myself that we couldn't lose that night. All of the motivation, all of the rage, all of the competitions with the French team. I felt it was finally materializing.

If I had to say when it all started, I would go all the way back to the 1997 U16 European championship. I shed my first tears, and it was my first sorrow with the French national team. I was 15, one year younger than everyone else. I was outmatched.

We were such a passionate and engaged team. We knew that the French team had never won the U16, and we wanted to be the first. We finished in fourth place, the best record for a French U16 team at the time. We wanted to go further. When we lost the semifinals against Russia, we were destroyed. The team was crying in the locker room. There were tears and rage. It really affected us. Too much, perhaps, because the next day we lost the game for the bronze medal against Israel, a team we had beaten in the pools. In that competition, for that group, it was either the gold medal or nothing. We were conditioned this way.

Paccelis Morlende, a shooting guard, was the star of that team. He was in the top five of the tournament, along with

Cédric Sinitambirivutin, Guy Guedegbe, Olivier Mognon, and Ahmed Fellah. We had played a huge game against Spain in the quarterfinals. In the semifinals against Russia, Andreï Kirilenko was really advanced. He was a monster. It was my first big loss wearing the blue jersey. It really hurt me and made an impression on me. But it was also the beginning of my intense love story with the French national team.

After that U16 tournament, I was overwhelmed. I felt a need to relive those moments and to share those emotions again. It was a passion of mine. I loved it. I hadn't even come to terms with that defeat, but I already knew that I wanted to win something with the French national team. That's where it all began.

The French national team also gave me the opportunity to travel and open my horizons. I only knew Normandy. Thanks to the drafts, I was able to explore a lot of other countries. When you're 14 or 15 years old, those kinds of experiences are irreplaceable.

The U16 was my baptism with the French national team, but it wasn't my first tournament. My first tournament with the French national team was in 1996, a few months earlier, in Bellegarde. We were preparing for the U16. That's when I started showing what I was capable of. The French team already had two good point guards, Guy Guedegbe and Ahmed Fellah. When I got there, I was the little "82." All of the others were born in 1981. I was the third-string point guard, the little new kid. During the training, I would earn my spot and become the starting point guard in the U16 championship.

I Made Myself a Promise in 2000

I can't explain the relationship, the connection, that I have with the French national team. It lit a fire within me, and it has never gone out, despite my NBA wins and a decent amount of losses with the French team. I always had great summers and experienced incredible personal adventures with my coaches and teammates. It was always a good time. I was happy to see Boris, Ronny, and Gaëtan Muller again. We had a good group.

When we won the U18 championship in 2000, I promised myself that I would come back to France every summer until we won the first gold medal in the history of French basketball for an international championship. It's a promise I kept for many years.

Every summer, it was like a family. I was happy to see the physical therapist and the doctor again. That's why I always said that I had two families: the Spurs during the year, and the French national team during the summer. I couldn't see myself not going to see my "second family" in the summer.

With time you develop your little habits. We often did the same tournaments and went to the same places. It created a kind of stability. It also allowed me to stay in shape and not be passive during the summer. Very early on, I got used to playing year-round. Even so, when I skipped the 2010 FIBA World championship and the 2014 World Cup, I was also being reasonable and not risking a huge injury. I could feel when my body was tired, and when enough was enough. At the time, I played 35-36 minutes per game in the NBA. With the Spurs, we played until the end of June, or close to it. Meanwhile, the others finished mid-April, and had two more months of vacation than I did. At some point, you have to know how to stay fit, because it's hard to always keep going and going and going. Throughout my international career, I always favored European championships. World championships aren't important. All the NBA players avoided the World championships.

Compared to soccer, our World Cup was like the Olympics. So I decided to participate in the European championships. I wanted to try to break records and become the person who has played the most, a record I hold today after eight EuroBaskets. I was the tournament's all-time leading scorer with 1,104 points, before Pau Gasol surpassed me in 2017. If we qualified for the Olympics, I would play, but I wouldn't play in the World championships because no one cares about them.

At the time, I was the only NBA player on the French national team who made it far in the playoffs. It was often over for the teams Boris and Ronny played for by mid-April. Since the beginning of my career, the Spurs made it to the playoffs every year, and very often, we went far. If you add up all of the games and all of the minutes I've played compared to the other players on the French team, it's substantial. That's why, in 2010 and 2014, I decided not to play. I had injured myself in 2006 right before the World championships, and I wasn't able to compete. But I was there. I had done all of the practice games before missing the tournament.

From 2000 to 2016, I came back every summer with two exceptions. When you know about the career I had with the club, you know it's a lot. Luckily, Vincent Collet, who has been the head coach since 2009, would have me rest often during training. If there were 10 practice games, I only played in seven.

My first selection with the French national team was against Turkey, in Ankara, in November of 2000. When the coach, Alain Weisz, called me, I truly wasn't expecting it. I was 18 and had finally started playing in Pro A. I was starting in Paris, where Ron Stewart had given me the keys to the team. I had a good start to the season, but I didn't think I'd join the French national team right away. Especially since they already had Antoine Rigaudeau and Laurent Sciarra and the team had just won the Olympic silver medal in Sydney. In my opinion, they didn't need a point guard. But the coach called me anyway. At the time, I was so proud. I had just become U18 champion, my whole future was before me, and I immediately moved on to a higher level.

I Didn't Want the No. 9

Before leaving for Turkey, we all got together for training in Paris. I was really respectful, I appreciated every moment, and I told myself that I was playing with the big boys now. The U16 and U18 were awesome. I was just hoping that we could have the same experiences in the major league. During my first draft to the French national team, I shared a room with Vasco Evtimov. I would also share a room with him in the 2001 EuroBasket.

The atmosphere was sick in Ankara! I immediately felt that the French team games had another flavor, a different type of enthusiasm. You're playing for your country. It's not just a club, or a city, it's for a whole country. With the national anthem and the first tipoff, you can tell it's not the same as a simple friendly game.

During the game, I played for about 10 minutes, and I scored four points. It was a good start. I was simply happy to be put in the game. I wasn't sure I'd play. When the coach put me in, I did my Tony thing. I was aggressive, and I went to the paint.

On the other hand, my first game with the blue jersey in France didn't go so well. It was against Italy in Villeurbanne. Now that I think about it, it's funny that my first game with the French national team on home soil was at the Astroballe. I didn't score any baskets. As I was leaving, I told myself, "Okay! I've got a long way to go. It's going to take a while."

During the first round of drafts, I wanted to be patient. But when I was drafted in June of 2001, everything sped up. The coach told himself, "We're going to have the little kid play anyway!"

My first competition was the 2001 EuroBasket in Turkey. Laurent Sciarra was the first-string point guard, but I still played a lot, especially during the second week. After that EuroBasket, I knew that the next time I played with the French national team, I'd have a real role to play. During the first week of the 2001 EuroBasket, I played a little bit, but I felt like I was already ready. I had just been drafted to the NBA. I wanted to play. I wanted to show what I could do. I knew that if they gave me the chance, I'd pull it off.

On that team, there were the "old guys," but also my teammates with whom I'd played in Paris: Laurent Sciarra and "Juju" (Cyril Julian). It went well with "Risac" (Stéphane

Risacher), Laurent Foirest, and Alain Digbeu. It was a good group that had fun. Continuity is what I learned with the young players. Morning, noon, and night we would eat together, and practice was scheduled at various times. It was the same process. The games are just so much more important than they are at the U16 or U18 level. I knew how the French national team worked. I needed to get to know my teammates. Vasco and I laughed a lot in our room. That giant is a real character. Despite what people jokingly predicted at the time, he never devoured me. He's a really good guy.

The second week, I had a little more game time, and I told myself it was high-level. The NBA is definitely tough, but the European game has nothing to be ashamed of. When I finished the games during the second week, I told myself that it was okay. I could dominate at that level. But I couldn't do it by myself, I had to be part of the team. You need a team and a lot of other things to win. I saw that it was within my capacity, and that in three or four years I thought I could really dominate the game.

Gregg Popovich was there in the bleachers. We said hi to each other in passing, but he didn't want to disturb me during my competition. I knew he was there, watching and observing his future point guard. He didn't put any pressure on me. He had already seen me during the Summer League.

It was no longer a secret. He knew who I was. He drafted me. He wanted me. I had a good relationship with Alain Weisz. He knew the game of basketball really well. Our relationship was so good that he had wanted to put me at the top a little too quickly.

During the 2003 EuroBasket, I moved into another dimension. In 2002, we weren't in the World championships so there was no French national team. But between 2001 and 2003, a lot of things happened. I was an NBA champion, the starting point guard, and the second-highest scorer for the Spurs. My status had completely changed. Immediately I felt catapulted as the star of the French national team. My No. 9 jersey was for sale. I remember a conversation with Jean-Pierre De Vincenzi, the DTN (National Technical Director) at the time: "I don't want the No. 9 on the French national team. I want the No. 6."

During the 2001 EuroBasket, I wore No. 6. I could see myself playing my entire career wearing 9 for the Spurs and 6 for the French national team. I was fine with that. I explained it to Jean-Pierre, but he insisted, "No, Tony. You have to wear 9. Everyone wants to buy the No. 9. You can't do that!"

I had to accept, and it created some awkwardness with Tariq Abdul-Wahad, who wanted that number. Besides, it wasn't in line with my American mentality, where you're very respectful of the senior players. They're the ones who should choose their numbers first. Tariq already had the 9. He could keep it. I was happy with 6. It created useless tension, while the senior players were already waging their own little war with the DTN following the 1999 EuroBasket and the 2000 Olympic games in Sydney.

Then, during the EuroBasket, the fact that Alain Weisz named me captain also made me uncomfortable. Sure, I was an NBA champion, but I was only 21. I thought it was more fitting for Mous Sonko or Laurent Foirest, a senior player, to have that role. It seemed normal for me. When he made me captain at the beginning of the season, I told him it was too early.

"Wait, Tony, you're an NBA champion. Of course, you're ready, you have the status. It's up to you to take charge of the team. We know that it's going to be *your* French team, so you might as well get started right away!"

I gave in, but I knew it was going to be difficult. It was too early, and I didn't deserve it. I needed experience and to have played several seasons. Then again, once I had it, I tried to be worthy of it with my good traits and personality. When you're 21 years old and yell like the captain, although you haven't proven anything yet on the French national team, it can be taken badly. Sometimes I tried to take the floor, but it wasn't easy. I still felt the need to prove that I could play on the French team. At the time, I was focused on my performances and getting comfortable with my new NBA champion status, which involved my being there for all the games.

The arenas were packed, and people wore my jersey. All of that mattered too. We also had a super talented team. The 2003 team was a lot better than the one in 2013, which went on to become champions of Europe. The team was really talented, but team spirit is crucial.

The Day I Ruined Everything

We finished first in our group and blew everyone out of the water in the pool phase. In the quarterfinals, we killed Russia. In the semifinals, we were one possession away from the finals. If Jérôme Moïso had moved forward during the pick and roll, we would have won against Lithuania and we could have been champions of Europe.

There was also my slip in the middle of the court. The referee came up behind me. He barely touched me, but it was enough to make me hesitate. After that, I lost the ball. Of course, I felt responsible. It was difficult, but that's part of a player's evolution and growing career. Those moments helped me out later on. It's easy to talk about it now because I know what happened after. But in the moment, it's really tough to live with.

Afterward, I told myself that it was meant to happen, that I had to go through it in order to become the decisive player I would become during the following competitions, and to become a key player in 2009, 2011, and 2013.

I not only lost that ball in the semifinals, but later, during the game for third place against Italy, I also missed a shot that would have taken the game into overtime. During those two games, I had two great performances. I scored 24 points each time, but on those two key plays, I didn't deliver. That night after the game, I was really disappointed. I didn't understand. I was mad at myself. Even though I was still young, I should have finished the job.

I ruined everything during the game for third place and kept the team from the 2004 Olympic games in Athens. We were face-to-face with Italy, whom we had beaten by 30 points one week earlier. Still, we lost by two points on a simple zone defense. In the end, in 2003, we were kind of like the U16 in 1997. Either we're champions of Europe or we don't give a damn. That was the team's mentality. We kind of didn't care about that bronze medal. It was shameful.

We never should have lost that game for third place. I quickly felt that our hearts weren't in it. Because of my temper, I tried to make the game my own and be the savior. But it might not have been my role at the time. I felt that I didn't have a lot of support. The guys weren't mean to me.

Sonko, Digbeu, Dioumassi, and even Tariq were pretty cool. We didn't fight. Honestly, there weren't any cliques. We were together. But that happens on teams. When a player blows a fuse, it doesn't mean the team falls apart. The group was okay. It was the overall context that complicated things.

During the final games of the tournament, and in particular this one, some people thought that the team had given up on me. I don't think that was the case. The senior players were more furious with the Federation for things that had happened two years prior, before I was even there.

Aside from all of that, I was still disappointed to have thrown away a chance at a medal, the possibility of going to the Olympic games, and maybe even a European title. In hindsight, when you watched Lithuania that year, it was a team that had matured, and it was their time. Since then, despite good teams every year, Lithuania hasn't won anything else. But it was their time in 2003. We had to wait. That year, we didn't deserve to be champions of Europe, even though we had the talent and the team for it.

When we left Sweden after the tournament, in fourth place and without a medal, I felt empty. I knew I wasn't going to see the French national team for two years. It was going to be tough.

My Biggest Disappointment While Wearing Blue

I was dead tired when I got to EuroBasket 2005. I had just won my second NBA title and I had really marked the occasion. I was exhausted. I didn't play well in the first three games of the tournament—it was like I wasn't even there.

I'd made a mistake before this event. I'd overextended myself—especially in terms of press and too many sponsorship deals. I was everywhere: appearances, commercials, TV sets—and I was still making it to the exhibition games. I was going nonstop. So when I got to the EuroBasket, I was beat. I realized it right away, and it opened my eyes. I paced myself better going forward.

Still, the beginning of that completely failed tournament was the first time that I really felt the love and support of all my teammates, of the French national team, of everyone. There had probably been some recognition before that, but the fact that I was there for the French national team that summer after such a long year and an NBA title, I think my teammates really appreciated my presence.

Obviously, what we took away from that EuroBasket and what we'll remember forever, is losing to Greece in the semifinal 77–66. It was my biggest disappointment on the French national team. Even though the story ended rather well with a win against Spain and the bronze medal, even though I had a good second week, the 2005 tournament was a good lesson, a nice little wakeup call to remind me that I shouldn't take on too much.

It affected me personally. I had gotten there with a reputation—I was the team captain. There was no doubt about it. That was my team for the next 10 years, my French team, my generation. I had started the tournament by playing three bad games. My role as captain was off to a terrible start. In 2003, it wasn't even my team, and I was still voted one of the top five players of the EuroBasket. Then I started off 2005 like that…

I had had my own dreams, my own goals, but suddenly they all seemed far away. It was hard to take. If you screw up your first game you tell yourself, "Okay! That can happen to anyone." But I also messed up the second game. I was with Boris in the hotel room and was annoyed: "I'm known for getting right back on my feet after a bad game, for reminding everyone who I am!"

In my mind, it was impossible for me to lose the third game. But I screwed up that one too! I really started to go through a period of doubt. I had sucked for three games in a row. And not sucked for like eight points and two or three assists. No, I really sucked, like averaging three points a game and shooting 20 percent from the field.

There is suck and there is SUCK, and I SUCKED.

Those might have been the three worst games of my career with the French national team—and to top it off, they were all in a row. It was unreal. I had to get back on my feet.

The head coach, Claude Bergeaud, could see that I was exhausted. He took me out of the starting lineup for the next game. I understood the decision. So I was going to come off the bench, and I made it my mission to push myself. All in all, it worked. I got back on my feet and had a strong finish at the EuroBasket that year.

But my play at the beginning of that tournament continued to bother me. I was upset. We were in Belgrade, Serbia, a basketball country, and the atmosphere was incredible. I told myself the event was made for me. Not being up to snuff was really hard.

Then there was obviously the semifinal loss to Greece. That one will hurt forever. We should have been champions of Europe that year. We were stronger than Germany, whom we would have played in the final if we had beaten the Greeks. A lot stronger.

We were seven points ahead, with 44 seconds left in the game. How did we lose that game? I still ask myself this question. I remember making a three-pointer, and then the Greeks called a timeout. We were seven points ahead. When I made that shot, I told myself, "Okay, we're champions of Europe! We're going to kill Germany!" I didn't even say,

"We're in the finals." I was already convinced that we would win it all. At that time, Dirk Nowitzki was Germany's only standout player. He was all alone. I don't even know what Claude Bergeaud said during the timeout. I was in my own little world. In my mind, we were already champions of Europe. We had beaten the best team in the EuroBasket that year.

But Greece made a comeback. Theodoros Papaloukas had wild moves and Dimitris Diamantidis made a shot that came out of nowhere. I didn't blame anyone on the French team, because we had all made mistakes in those last 44 seconds, myself included. When Diamantidis made his shot, I told myself Greece was destined to win. A shot like that is clearly an act of fate.

I was dead tired, but I recovered very quickly. I told myself it just wasn't our time. Not yet. The defeat was hard to stomach, but we had the strength and the character to go for the bronze. We beat Spain, our most hated rival. I scored 25 points, we qualified for the World Cup, and we brought home the first French EuroBasket medal in 50 years. Granted, we didn't win it all in 2003 and 2005. We could have been champions of Europe, but I told myself that it was only a matter of time before we would win that title, and I had my entire future ahead of me.

The Birth of My Generation

Aside from those two personal and team disappointments, there was a magnificent moment during the 2005 EuroBasket: our win against Serbia, on their turf.

At the time, Serbia was the Spain of our generation. Everyone thought they would win the European championship. So when we finished third in our pool, in part because of my mistakes, and then we had to turn around and play Serbia, everyone thought it was over. Nothing was going our way.

The night before the game, we left Belgrade and headed to Novi Sad by bus. We still had hope, even if it was a small chance. We were not giving up. No one looked particularly happy, but Claude Bergeaud was calm and collected: "We don't have a big chance of winning, guys. We need to be aware of that. But if we play a good defensive zone, active ball movement, and successful shots, we have a small chance. If we're in the game during the fourth quarter, they'll start shaking in their boots."

Bergeaud might have been calm, but I was still reeling from my mistakes in the previous games.

We played zone for most of the game. Serbia dug in their heels. They were faltering. Sometimes teams crack under pressure on their home court. And they cracked. In fact, that game was the first huge win of our generation. We beat the

Serbs 74–71. Serbia had been the model team for years and defeating them was huge for us. I reconnected with myself during that game. I made my little signature move against Dejan Bodiroga. I was playing in the fourth quarter. I felt good. I kept coming back, and the team gained momentum. It was a perfect game for me. The atmosphere was wild. I was back in the groove.

When we got back to the locker room, we didn't stop yelling. We were all over the place. It was indescribable. No one had believed in us. It was such an improbable win. I believe this game was the birth of a new era for the French team. It was there that we showed what we were made of and proved, for the first time, that we could rise above adversity and win.

By the time we got to the semifinal against Spain, we had learned a lot from our 2003 EuroBasket experience and the mess we had made of that tournament. A repeat performance was not an option.

At dinner the night before the game, it was all anyone could talk about. No matter where I turned, I heard, "Do you remember 2003…We can't mess it up a second time…It's a medal, a nice little souvenir…We've never had a medal with the French national team…We need to bring one home." Granted, we had just taken a huge hit, but the disappointment from our loss to Greece went away much faster than the sting of our loss to Lithuania two years earlier. At dinner, everyone agreed. It's a bronze medal. We have to get it. It's important. It'll go down in history.

Beating Spain was a huge accomplishment for us, even if Pau Gasol didn't play in the tournament. For 15 years, Spain was our fiercest rival, our worst enemy. People often said if it hadn't been for that incredible generation of Spanish players, we might have dominated European basketball. But we didn't let that get us down. History would give us the gold medal in 2013. If that hadn't been the case, seeing Spain win again and again would have been infuriating. No one wants to come in second place for 10 years. But winning a European championship got rid of that feeling. Of course, had it not been for Spain, we could have won three more. But we reached the goal I had set for myself and my team: bring home the title for the first time in the history of French basketball.

Like Deschamps and Zidane

Even if the 2003 and 2005 tournaments were rather painful, I did not lose my motivation after those losses. But I became aware of one thing: when Antoine Rigaudeau, who had been the team captain in 2005, retired, I didn't want to be part of a French national team that only revolved around me.

I was young in 2003. I didn't dare say much. But in 2006, I had an entirely different approach. I was an NBA All-Star, and when I made it to the French team in the summer of 2006, I laid it out like this: "You want me to be captain, okay, no problem. I can play that part now. But I think it would be better if it were Boris. That will make two leaders at the head of the team."

The media talked about me constantly. For the good of the team, I felt it was better for someone else to be captain. I passed the torch to Boris, because I knew that he could be a very good captain, and he proved it for the next 10 years. That system, with Boris as the captain and me as the leader on the court, worked really well for years. I imagined us to be a little like the French national football team in 1998, with Didier Deschamps as captain and "Zizou" as the leader on the pitch. I even used that example with my coach, Claude Bergeaud.

Had it not been for an injury, 2006 would have been my only world championship. During the practice game against Brazil, my finger got caught in Tiago Splitter's jersey. I immediately felt the pain. I was sure it was just a sprain and would feel a little better after I iced it. But the next day at practice when I tried to shoot, I couldn't put any weight on my finger. I couldn't feel the ball. I had X-rays taken and found out I had fractured my finger. I might have been able to play by taping my index and middle fingers together, but it was risky.

I sent the X-rays to the Spurs, as an NBA player should do when injured, and they immediately refused to let me play: "We're paying him I don't know how many millions of dollars. The answer is no." If the Spurs hadn't objected, I would have tried to play. But they didn't want me to, and it wasn't even worth further discussion. In the NBA, that's the rule. When you're injured, you're not allowed to play. If your club doesn't want you to play, you don't play.

So I missed the World championships. I was disappointed at the time, but I didn't have a choice. World championships weren't my priority, anyway. My main focus was winning a gold medal in the EuroBasket and participating in the Olympics. Sure, I had gone through all of the training and I had wanted to play with my team, but it didn't affect me too much.

I stayed with my teammates during the first game of the World championships. Especially since we played Argentina and Manu Ginobili was there.

Afterward, I immediately went back to San Antonio. The Spurs wanted to see my finger as quickly as possible. It eventually healed, but it's still crooked. When I see the fingers of other NBA players, I feel I've made out okay after a 20-year career.

A Huge Failure in 2007

I returned to the French national team for the 2007 EuroBasket in Spain. The first part of the tournament was good. We beat big teams like Italy and Germany. Then it was time for the quarterfinals against Russia.

In those tournaments, if you lose the quarterfinal game, it sets a tone for the remaining games. We lost to Russia 75–71. They would go on to win the title, while we struggled to play the way we had during the first week. The team was okay with the loss, and everyone was fine. It's just that we weren't winning the games. Sometimes it's as simple as that. After the quarterfinals, Croatia killed us 86–69 and Slovenia kicked our asses 88–74! We finished in eighth place. We weren't good at all.

The 2007 EuroBasket was the worst result of my generation. With losses to Croatia and Slovenia, I missed out on the Olympics again. I started to tell myself I would never get there. You have to land the shots in order to win, and we didn't land any.

Agonizing and Free Throws

Throughout my career, I was a 75 percent free throw shooter. A point guard usually hits between 80 percent and 85 percent. Let's just say I did a decent amount of overthinking on the line. I agonized a good deal over free throws. I wanted my movements to be too perfect and I always missed one. However, during my better seasons—2012, 2013, 2014—I managed to stay centered and hit 80 percent. During my best season, 2012–13, I hit over 84 percent. But in 2007, in those last few seconds of the quarterfinals against Russia, I made two of four and Bobo made zero of three. And that's how the game ended.

In terms of results, the 2007 EuroBasket was a failure. But on a personal level, it was important. It was the first tournament with the French national team where I averaged 20 points a game and set a personal record for points scored in a European championship game, with 36 points against Italy. That EuroBasket gave me confidence for the future and made me want to keep coming back for more.

In 2007, after my first-round record-setting game against Italy, everyone was talking about "Parker addiction." I had just become an NBA champion, an All-Star, and the MVP of the Finals. I didn't worry too much about the rest. Maybe even in the euphoria of my NBA season, I could see myself donning a hero's cape. But I wasn't really looking for it. In fact, I saw my team was in trouble, and my natural reaction was to try to save them. Maybe I wanted to play that role too much in 2007.

Carte Blanche

After another disappointment with the French national team, I found motivation in the challenge that lay before me.

So far, my path in the NBA had been an easy road. With the French team, on the other hand, nothing came easy. We were really going to have to work hard for the trophy. But I wasn't discouraged. The repeated failures had the opposite effect on me. Instead of telling myself, "I give up. I'm fed up with the French team," I decided I wouldn't retire until I'd won gold. I was convinced that we were going to achieve something. We just needed to keep playing.

In 2008, we were the lowest of the low. As they say in English, we hit rock bottom. That summer, we had to go through the EuroBasket qualifiers, and we didn't even qualify. Not many NBA players came in 2008, so it was basically Ronny Turiaf and me with a B-team. We did what we could to keep the French team afloat.

It's funny, because I wasn't supposed to go to the 2008 qualifiers, either. I was on vacation in Los Angeles when Ronny called me and said, "No, TP, you can't do this to me. You can't leave me all alone!" He poured his heart out to me, and I gave in.

It was a really strange season, and our living conditions were not optimal. For our game in Kiev, Ukraine, the hotel wasn't great. We were two to a room. My feet stuck out of the bed. It was okay for me, but for guys who were over 6-foot-5, it was uncomfortable.

You really had to be motivated to play. We were far from the bright lights, far from everything, at the very bottom of the barrel. But once again, that feeling motivated me to stay the course. I told myself that someday when we finally won, it would mean more to me and I would really enjoy it given what we'd gone through.

In 2008, the head coach was Michel Gomez. It was a strange choice. He hadn't coached in a long time. Everyone introduced him as the incredible coach from the 1990s, but the gap between 1990 and 2008 was pretty obvious.

Of course, there were disagreements with Michel. In fact, I had trouble understanding him. He gave us a lot of freedom in the game. We would ask for defensive guidance, and he would reply, "Do what you want. For the pick and roll, go with your gut."

I had left a very well-defined game plan with Popovich, where we had the best defense in the NBA. I got to the French national team, and we could do what we wanted. It was questionable coaching. You can't tell the players to do what they want. They have to know what they're doing, where they're going, and how they're going to defend. You have to decide on a strategy.

It was really difficult to get used to Gomez's coaching style. He gave me carte blanche. I had my biggest offensive successes and set my record for the most points on the French national team: 37 points against Turkey in Limoges. I was really in the mode of feeling like I had to save the team.

The guys were good sports. We laughed a lot, and the mood on the team was good. But they didn't have the experience, and they had never played at that level. Against the EuroLeague players, there was a decent amount of action. Dounia Issa and Yakhouba Diawara were on the team. It was also the first draft for Nando De Colo, who was really young. There was Stephen Brun, Steed Tchicamboud, and William Gradit.

We gave a good fight, and we qualified in the last game against Turkey in Limoges. With the last shot, actually. After that play, the Turks double-teamed me. I passed the ball to Nando, and he made the play. He penetrated and passed to Yakhouba, who was open and took a three-pointer. He didn't make it, but it was a good shot. There were a lot of rookies, and the team didn't have any experience with that. I never regretted having played that season. I preferred coming to help out the French team over doing nothing on vacation. Each experience is useful and keeps you motivated.

Mafia's Magical Effect

The following year, in 2009, more younger players arrived. For Nicolas Batum and Antoine Diot, it was their big debut, their first draft. I told myself, "Okay, they're talented, but it's going to take some time before they can help us out in a competition."

However, we had a good EuroBasket that year. We won all our games but lost to Spain in the quarterfinal. In the first round, the Spanish star Pau Gasol was hurt, and Spain had finished fourth in their group. We had finished first in ours, with a 6–0 record. Yet Gasol reappeared in the quarterfinal, and with him back on the court, Spain had a wicked game. We were never lucky when it came to Spain.

Nonetheless, I left the competition feeling like we were going to be able to achieve something. We had the right young players, and the team's chemistry was taking shape. I could tell they had a good attitude and were going to fit in well with the older players. We finished fifth in that EuroBasket, at 8–1. I could see great prospects for the future.

The same year, there was another game against Greece in the first round that got a lot of buzz. It's a funny story. Before the game, we had already qualified, and we knew that if we won, we'd likely have to play against Spain, our old rivals, in the quarterfinals. Should we play to win? Should we lose? There really was no consensus. Honestly, we all hesitated.

On the one hand, we didn't want to overthink it. That never works. On the other hand, we told ourselves, "Come on, let's analyze it anyway." We couldn't reach a clear-cut decision.

At halftime, Vincent Collet, the new head coach, still hadn't taken a stance. Even I, as the leader, was hesitant on the court. I never said to my teammates, "Let's win it," or "Let's lose." It was not easy to play a game like this.

When Nando made the final shot for a 71–69 victory, we simply told ourselves that we were going to play Spain in the quarterfinals, and that was not a walk in the park. It was kind of a shame, because we could have had a gold medal in the championship. When we saw that Serbia, a super young team, was second and Greece third, and they had dangled a carrot in front of us, it was clearly a shame.

But in 2009, we had a solid foundation. Up until that point, we were missing the pieces we needed to win the title. Hope was reborn with Nicolas Batum, a great forward, and Antoine Diot, the perfect complement for me at the forefront. I took them under my wing. I took them out to eat and hung out with them. I constantly talked to them and explained the importance of the French national team. You joined the team to win a title, not to go on vacation or shine individually. We were there for the team and for our country. We were there to win something together for France.

Bobo and I always tried to make everyone comfortable. We tried to bridge the gap between the NBA players who were earning a lot of money and those who were living on their French national team salary. Bobo and I often socialized with them during training camp so that we could all be together and mingle.

In 2008, when I arrived to prepare for the qualifiers, I started a FIFA video game tournament and gave everyone a PlayStation. In 2009, I introduced the game *Mafia* to the team. We didn't want everyone taking off to their rooms after dinner. Boris had started coffee meetings after each meal, and afterward we would all play together. Thanks to that, we took the time to get to know one another. It was the opposite of my arrival in 2001. We would eat together and then everyone would go up to their rooms.

You can't force people to become friends. Bonding either happens naturally or it doesn't. Starting in 2009, the French national team had a real familial atmosphere. With the Spurs, everyone had a very different background. Manu came from Argentina, Tim came from the Virgin Islands, and I was from France and Belgium. How could we know that the three of us were going to create something special that the whole team would endorse? We spent time together. Pop was really into that. He held team dinners after road games so we could hang out off the court. That's something that's usually not done in the NBA.

The first time I played *Mafia* was in Los Angeles. At the time I was married to Eva Longoria. A group of actors we frequently saw had started the game: Jennifer Lopez (who was really into it), Terry Crews, Amaury Nolasco (from *Prison Break*), and a few from the *Desperate Housewives* cast too. It was really the perfect game to get to know people. Everyone talked to one another, and it made everyone comfortable.

From 2009 to 2016, the game was an important part of the culture of the French national team. No one ever refused to participate. It was part of our normal routine. When Boris and I first started the game, there was still a difference between the NBA stars and the other players, and no one dared say no. But right away, the whole group came together, and everyone played willingly.

I even brought it to my youth basketball camps. We played huge games of *Mafia* with over 60 people. It became a tradition. In fact, when we became champions of France with ASVEL in 2016, we were all at the hotel the night before the decisive match for the title. After dinner, Charles Kahudi openly asked me, "Hey, TP, do you want to play *Mafia*?" We played a game that included all of the team's players as well as the physical therapists, doctors, and coaches. We played until almost midnight. It relaxed everyone. What a laugh we had, and the next day we won Game 5 and were champions of France.

Captain, But Not Head Coach

I started out on the French national team as the little guy, the young kid, the rookie. Little by little, I took on more responsibilities until I became the leader. At the time, the French team was basically on my side. But I never chose the team, or even a player, and I never influenced the head coach. When they asked for my opinion, which Vincent Collet did, I gave it. He also asked Boris Diaw and Flo Pietrus, but it never went further than that. Vincent Collet, Claude Bergeaud, Alain Weisz, and Michel Gomez were the four coaches I had on the French national team, and they were in charge of their teams. I always respected their choices. I never imposed anything whatsoever. It's important for a coach to make his or her own decisions. It's respect for the profession.

Starting in 2009, there was a lot of reflection about the game on the French team. Vincent Collet told me, "Tony, I know you can score 20 or 30 points per game, but if you want to win something with the French national team, you have to change the way you do it. Have the team play more during the first half, and if you have to, take the game on for yourself during the second half."

That's when I really started becoming a leader. From that moment on, I started making the rounds in the hotel rooms to make sure everyone was okay. I sacrificed my game to give my teammates more confidence. It was never a source of frustration for me. I wanted to win with the French national team so badly. We didn't win in 2003, 2005, or 2007. So I realized it might be necessary to change certain things. I was open to that. As a result, my best EuroBaskets were in 2009, 2011, and 2013.

Making the rounds to the rooms came naturally. I didn't have a set plan. I did it on the fly. Of course, some discussions touched me more than others, like with Nico Batum during the 2013 EuroBasket. He wasn't really okay during the competition. He was dealing with some personal issues, and he wasn't doing very well. Before the finals, I went to see him in his room.

"You know, Nico, up until now we've done what we had to do. Everyone in the EuroBasket has their moment at some point and has a great performance. And for you it's going to be the finals. All we need is you! Okay, you're frustrated with this EuroBasket, but if you have a great game in the finals, people will only remember that game and the gold medal.

They will have forgotten that you sucked during the entire EuroBasket!"

Obviously that last sentence was to diffuse the tension, but it did the trick.

During these discussions, you have to be sensitive and considerate. Private lives are never easy to manage. I would often tell the guys who had just joined the French national team that they had to take time to rest. When you play basketball, you play hard. That's what you love to do and you put the rest aside.

When I was going through my divorce from Eva, I was voted best player of the week, despite the personal stress I was under. I appreciated the recognition. That only happened to me eight or nine times throughout my career. Sometimes it's important to be able to compartmentalize. That doesn't mean you're not allowed to be sad. But when you're on the court, you have to get the job done.

In the first half of the 2013 EuroBasket final, Nico scored 17 points. He was incredible, and he's the one who got us on track.

Another conversation made an impression on me. It was in 2009, before the game against Belgium at the EuroBasket tournament. We were in the locker room. It was only Ronny, Bobo, and me. We looked at each other and said it was impossible not to qualify for the EuroBasket. In Pau, we won the game by 30 points and had an unbelievable celebration with the crowd after the game.

In order to break the vicious cycle with the Greeks, I also talked to Nando De Colo before the game against Greece in 2011. At the time, Nando was our sixth man, and I wanted to remind him how precious he was to us. And he had been really good during that game.

The best French national team I've played with was the 2011 team. We were really solid that year. We only lost to Spain in the finals. Twice, actually, but the first loss was in the pool stage and was low-stakes, even though it was undoubtedly a heated European rivalry.

All of the stars were there and on top of their game. Joakim Noah was with us, and that changed things. He brought incredible energy. He's really a special and unique player. It's a shame he didn't compete in more tournaments with us. If Joakim had been with us at the 2012 Olympic games, I think we would have beaten Spain in the quarterfinals. Of course, I tried to convince him to come back. But I can understand how he felt about playing with the French national team. I'm familiar with the stakes and the risks of playing with your national team when you've signed a contract with the NBA. If the guys want to rest their bodies during the off-season, I can't help but respect that.

In 2012, after our loss in the Olympic quarterfinals against Spain, I really started speaking up. It wasn't so much a rant as it was a rallying cry. We had been in the lead for the entire game. We deserved to win it. I could see the whole team was disappointed and dejected in the locker room. I asked to schedule a meeting the very next day and I told them, "Guys, I know we're all disappointed. We feel like we can't do it, that we'll never beat Spain. But we can't give up. We all have to come back next year. We can't leave like that. No one should retire. We have to keep going."

The following year was 2013, the EuroBasket, and the title. I often tease Ronny, who didn't listen to me and retired before the EuroBasket. "You see, Ronny? I told you not to retire. I told you it would happen!"

Our Greatest Rival

Although 2013 was a big milestone for me, it was also a strange year. The Spurs had just finished the NBA Finals with a painful loss to Miami in seven games. In terms of business, I had just signed a big deal with Peak and was in full swing.

After we lost to Miami, I kind of hesitated to go play with the French national team. I was really tired at the end of that season. I was the best NBA point guard that year. I don't think I had ever played basketball that well. As they say, I was at the top of my game.

So I almost sat out the season with the French team. I was really tired and the loss to Miami was hard to swallow. There were also a lot of defections on the French team, especially within the interior defense. We were wiped out. We had rookies in the interior: Joffrey Lauvergne and Johan Petro. No disrespect to them, but it was looking a little complicated. I waffled back and forth for a week, and in the end, as I often do, I motivated myself to take the risk: "Come on, let's go. It's on!"

I was tired, but I dealt with it. I spent more time in the weight room. I did all the exercises carefully in order to avoid any injuries. That was my priority: one practice per day and slow, careful training. Vincent Collet and the entire medical staff were always very considerate of that with me during each summer. I was always the last one to finish my season, and they took good care of me. Without a modified schedule, it would have been impossible to train and play nonstop.

The 2013 EuroBasket is pretty symbolic of my journey with the French national team. We struggled during training. We struggled in the first round of the tournament. Our performance was up and down. We lost the opening game to Germany 80–74. In the second round, Serbia kicked our asses 77–65, and I told myself that it was going to be a long road, that we just weren't in the zone. We were a little out of sorts for that tournament. Ironically, 2013 was the year I least expected us to win.

At the same time even when we were in a tough spot, I never once gave up. I simply told myself that it was going to be hard. We didn't play well the first week. The team didn't click. But we had a defensive base, and it only took one game for things to shift quickly in our favor.

It was the quarterfinals against Slovenia, a home game for them, that put us back in the zone and helped us regain our confidence. It was our benchmark game. The atmosphere was electric. It was incredible. Slovenia was completely behind its team. But we were super calm and sure of our strength. We knew that up until that point, we hadn't been playing at our usual level. In 2007 and 2009, we had screwed up the big games. I kept repeating to everyone that the time was now, in the quarterfinals, to make a difference. I was sure that our past experiences would help us.

Honestly, the 2013 team wasn't as strong as we had been in 2011. We lost three games during that EuroBasket, and yet we were champions of Europe that year. We won the games we needed to win.

That was the year I had my most famous rant during halftime in the semifinals against Spain. All those years of frustration came out in one speech. We were down by 14.

I didn't recognize my team. We were playing like we were afraid of Spain.

"It's impossible to talk about a gold medal if we're scared of winning it. They're dominating us because they think we're shit. You can see it on their faces, they think we're shit."

Everything came out at once. As we made our way to the locker room, I knew I was going to take the floor. The coaches were in the middle of setting up their own thing, but I was on a roll. I just spoke to them from my heart. I was filled with rage and many other emotions. I kept telling myself if we didn't win now, we would never win. Every summer we worked our asses off to try to accomplish something. I didn't want to see us throw away our hard work because we were afraid. At the end of the day, someone had to lose. That's just sports. If the opponent is stronger, you shake hands and try again another day. But in those semifinals, I knew we had to come out on top. I couldn't allow Spain to dominate us like that. Every emotion I was feeling came pouring out at once.

And it worked. The French team did a 180 in the second half of the game, and we won the semifinals. It was my favorite game with the French team, a 75–72 victory, all of those emotions I let out during halftime, my individual performance with 32 points scored, the three-pointer I made to push us over the top with 1:30 left on the clock. I exploded with determination and rage during that game. Even when

Rudy Fernandez blocked me on the last play of regulation time, it didn't bother me. A great defense, and we moved on to something else.

Overtime was intense. No one scored a point for three minutes. It was a wild game. Then, Antoine Diot and I made eight out of eight free throws. It was our time. We got the job done.

One image from this game really stands out, the best moment of my entire career in the blue uniform: someone snapped a picture of me hugging Nando and Antoine Diot so tightly as the buzzer went off. You can see the intense happiness on my face. Just thinking about it gives me goosebumps. It's difficult to explain the emotions I felt in that moment. So many things that were inside of me came out all at once. You could see it all on my face. Then there was the certainty that we were going to be crowned champions of Europe.

I was so happy. I made so many sacrifices for the French national team. I took so many risks, doing those summers right after really long seasons with the Spurs. I could have injured myself any number of times. So I was happy and relieved to be finally rewarded. There are a lot of athletes who reach that point. They work hard and never experience that kind of bliss. Not everyone gets that privilege. That night, I finally achieved it.

Constantly losing to Spain over the years had really taken its toll on us. In my opinion, that win held every possible emotion for the French national team. It was almost more powerful than winning the title the next day. I knew that the final was just a formality.

To be clear, I never really hated Spain. In the end, it was thanks to them that the French players continued to push ourselves. Our desire to beat them forced us to keep improving. Spain had been a real motivator for us. In order to become the best, a team needs an opponent whose strength constantly pushes and challenges, like Nadal and Federer, Magic Johnson and Larry Bird. All throughout my career on the French national team, there weren't really any European point guards who pushed me to my limits. At the time, I dominated the point guard position in Europe, and I was winning NBA titles. But I no longer cared about individual goals. I wanted to win with the French team, and I wanted to beat Spain.

Every summer, when I returned to the French team as either NBA champion or Finals MVP, there were expectations. For me, it was the same pressure I had with the Spurs—I had to win a title. It's a normal kind of pressure. We undoubtedly had the best generation there'd ever been in French basketball, and people wanted a title. It was understandable. Sure, we had won medals, but we knew everyone was waiting for the gold medal. I took on the challenge.

At the Top of My Game

Before our game against Spain, I stood in a corner of the arena and watched Lithuania qualify for the finals. They were so happy to make it, they were celebrating and jumping all over. We felt relief and joy when we beat Spain, but we were past that phase. We had already played in the finals in 2011. Now we had to win.

During dinner that night, all we could talk about was the final: "It's good to go. We're going to destroy Lithuania. We didn't kill Spain just to lose in the finals." We were pumped up, but we had our eyes on the ultimate goal. No one partied. The FFBB (French Federation of Basketball) didn't have a celebration. We were focused.

The following day, we won 80–66. We were on a mission. I didn't even need to give a speech to motivate my team. I had said it all during halftime of the semifinals.

What was nice about those finals is that I had time to enjoy the title. That was significant. I was on the bench for the last five minutes. I was able to experience the moment and hug everyone. I remember hugging Vincent Collet, Flo Piétrus, and Bobo. We looked at each other like, "That's it! We made it!" The pressure floated away. That moment was magnificent, even if it was less intense than our win against Spain. Because we knew that after a few minutes of pure pleasure, we would finally have that beautiful medal.

On the bus, we played all the "champion" songs. The privilege of winning is rare in sports, and being able to share that with your family and friends makes it even better. When we got to the hotel, the lobby was packed with all our family and friends. We all ate together at the hotel before going to a club. I didn't really drink much that night. I was more nostalgic. We spent a lot of time reminiscing about the stories that stood out the most for us throughout our years in blue. The emotions stayed with me for a while, throughout the entire year that followed in the NBA.

That year, in two months' time, I experienced a huge emotional roller coaster. In June, we lost to Miami in the NBA Finals. It was the biggest loss of my career. And at the end of the summer, I followed it with the greatest joy of my career.

When I came back to practice with the Spurs at the end of September, I was champion of Europe and on cloud nine. Pop immediately threw us back into the drama of our loss to Miami. From the first day of training camp, he had us watch Game 6 of the Miami series and the dramatic ending. I was happy with my gold medal, and I showed it to the guys. I was super excited. Then, seeing those images, I suddenly said to myself, "Oh yeah. That's right. We lost that one."

Regardless, the EuroBasket title gave me a positive energy for the whole year with the Spurs. I didn't allow myself to be affected by that 2013 NBA Finals loss. On the contrary, I kept the momentum from the European title with the French national team. When I became NBA champion in 2014, it was a pinnacle for me. Champion of Europe immediately followed by NBA champion. There was no better feeling. I was at the very top of my game.

For me, that 2013 title was the culmination of 10 years of work with the French team. I wouldn't change my history with the French national team for anything in the world. I was happy to have gone through all those phases and endured all those failures to end up there. It meant even more because I went through it all with Ronny and Bobo. After the warm-up, in the locker room, or before hitting the court, we would wait until everyone left, and the three of us would reminisce, talk about what we had experienced, what we went through to get there, and why we made all those sacrifices. It was the good kind of nostalgia, and as the years passed, we kept telling ourselves, "It's almost over! We really need to enjoy these final moments."

Ronny wasn't on the team in 2013, but Bobo and I were really nostalgic during the competition. If I hadn't won that gold medal with the French team, I might not be retired today. Seriously, I would have considered it a failure. Whenever I would have had to talk about my career, it would have hurt to say I didn't win with the French team. I really wanted to win something. That's why I was able to retire peacefully. I managed to do everything I wanted to do in basketball, and even more. I could never have imagined that.

The title with the French team in 2013 was definitely the one I enjoyed the most. It was the one I waited the longest for too. That day, a very heavy weight suddenly lifted off my shoulders. I tend to say that it was my most successful EuroBasket. I say that because we went all the way, but in 2011, my performance was also very consistent. I finished both of those EuroBaskets as the best point guard. I think I also had a very successful tournament in 2009 as well.

After winning the 2013 title, I probably approached my last two international competitions with the French team a little differently. I started playing with the feeling that I had accomplished what I came to do. For me, those last two tournaments were bonuses.

I could have retired from international play in 2013. That would have happened if the 2015 EuroBasket hadn't taken place in France. But I said, "I'm going to play for my country, in my country." Since we almost qualified for the Olympics, I pushed on a little further to the 2016 Olympic games in Rio. After that, it was time to walk away.

Regretting the 2015 EuroBasket in France

In 2015, for the first time in the history of French basketball, we were favored to win at the start of a European championship. There were huge expectations each time I played for the French national team. The 2015 EuroBasket was more intense because it was in France, but the pressure was the same. As the reigning champions, we knew going in that if we left without the gold medal, the tournament would be considered a failure.

I didn't play much in the first five games, and I truly regret that. We played against five average teams, and I felt like I never really found my stride. When we got to the quarterfinals, I said to myself, "Okay, Tony. You're on! You're going to play for 35 minutes. You have to get going now."

But I was 33 at the time. All the minutes in the NBA and with the French national team had piled up. I was having a minor shoulder issue, which happens to a lot of players. I was definitely a little tired.

We made it to the semifinals and played Spain again. And then, disappointment! I didn't play the game everyone was expecting me to play. I always work toward being at my best level every time. But I did not play a good game against

Spain. We lost 80–75 in overtime. I went into the game knowing if we beat Spain, we would be taking home another gold medal, but it didn't happen. We screwed it up.

Coming in third felt like a failure, but not completely. It's really hard to win a medal in a European championship. Ten years before, when my generation and I came on the scene, winning a gold medal was improbable. When we won the bronze medal in 2005, that hadn't happened since 1959. Ten years later, when we won the bronze again, people said, "Well, it's not the gold medal!" In 10 years, those expectations showed how much the French team had grown. We had come so far that the standards had changed. A bronze medal was no longer good enough.

On a personal level, the 2015 EuroBasket is still a failure for me because I didn't play up to my standards. It happens. Pau Gasol had sucked in the 2014 World Cup in Spain against the French national team, and the following year he scored 40 points and killed us. That time, I was the one who wasn't good.

The problem was, it happened *in* France. People have asked me several times if Vincent Collet should have taken me out of the game earlier because I wasn't at my best. They've asked if he wasn't a little cowardly in that moment. That's just the media looking for a story. If I were the coach and I had a player who carried my team for 10 years, I would tell myself he'd get through it, like he had done throughout his entire career. It had been the same thing with the Spurs. Pop had never taken me out because of a bad start. He knew that sooner or later I'd get back in the game. A coach will fight to the death with his best players. But I couldn't get it going during that game.

In hindsight, there were still good times. The atmosphere was incredible. It was wild to play in France, in the football stadium in Lille. It was a superb competition. A bronze medal is still a medal. You can't turn your nose up at a medal. I didn't even have to give a big speech after the semifinals loss. I could tell the guys weren't giving up and were motivated to go get the bronze medal. We all knew it wasn't possible to finish the tournament on French soil without a medal.

I was overcome with nostalgia on the podium. It was my last EuroBasket. The crowd was incredible. I'm still very much grateful for the experience.

Lastly, the Olympic Games

The Olympics Qualification Tournament (OQT) followed in June 2016. It was out of the question for me to end my career with an OQT in the Philippines. I was motivated like never before in the deciding match against Canada. I wanted to go to Rio and finish my international career in the Olympics.

I was so happy to be in the Philippines for that competition. I brought my family, my brothers, my friends. Everyone was there to see me play one last time for the French national team. It was a really special tournament for me. I had wanted to enjoy it and it was a great trip. We laughed a lot.

The games were awesome. We played against the Philippines, in their packed arena. The atmosphere was sick. Then, in the finals against Canada, I was face-to-face with Steve Nash. It was really great. I loved that tournament. It was really meaningful to me. It was the twilight of my international career. I knew it. Everyone knew it. I was completely in the competition because the stakes were huge: qualifying for the Olympics. I really reveled in every moment.

However, the tournament had started really early and Axelle was in the last few weeks of her pregnancy with Liam. It wasn't easy. I went back and forth between the Philippines and San Antonio. Once we had qualified for the Olympics, I went back to San Antonio for my son's birth before meeting up with the team in Brazil. Luck was with me then too. The timing was perfect. Liam was born at the right time. Good job, Liam!

There wasn't a lot of focus on the game against Canada because it was just a qualifier, but it really was an important game. Canada had a strong team. Those finals, it was a huge deal. I came out with a vintage performance like the good old days. Recovering from the 2015 EuroBasket failure, coming back with a good performance and qualifying for the Olympics with the French team at 34 years old made me so happy. I scored 26 points during that game, which hadn't happened since the 2013 EuroBasket.

But hey, that's a sidenote, because at that point in my career, it no longer mattered to me to have that kind of individual performance. Honestly, I had nothing left to prove with the French national team. I was simply happy because we qualified for the 2016 Olympics. But emotionally, the OQT was a richer experience for me than the Olympic tournament in Rio.

I was super happy to be playing in the Olympic games, but my second child had just been born. I saw him for one day and then had to leave the next day. But from then on my life had changed. I had a child, my brothers had kids, and they could no longer travel as freely as they once had. I made the decision to go to Rio alone. I told myself that if everyone couldn't be there, I wasn't just going to bring my mother or father. Either everyone came or no one did.

The story ended, symbolically, in the quarterfinals against our biggest rival, Spain. I have no regrets. Spain was simply better than us in that game, and we lost 92–67.

You have to leave at some point, and for me, the Olympics was a good exit. We played an admirable tournament. The United States, Serbia, Spain, and Australia were in front of us, four of the greatest teams in the world. There was no shame in losing in the quarterfinals, in finding ourselves behind those four teams, and in being one of the eight best nations in the Olympics that year.

That's why I don't understand why our tournament in Rio has always been criticized. I think it's part of the French mindset. We always want to nitpick. France had set the bar so high that because we didn't win a medal, everyone decided there was a problem with the team. But there was no problem. It's just not realistic to think we can win medals every year. The French national team won four medals in five years. This time around, we didn't win one. That can happen, right? Spain kicked our asses in the quarterfinals, and maybe that's why people suspected a lack of commitment. But I don't think that was the case. We lost to Spain in the quarterfinals and that's it.

It was my last international competition. I had the same motivation I'd always had. I had broken my big toe before the game and probably shouldn't have played. Especially since the Spurs didn't want me playing while injured. But there was no way I wasn't going to play in that game.

During the game, I knew it would be my last time on the court with the French national team. I am so proud of all those years that I didn't want to let a game or a final loss tarnish that incredible experience and define my international career. I knew that I would stop playing after Rio. I had already made peace with myself. I didn't have a particular emotion during the final minutes of the game. In that moment, I was mainly proud. Proud of the French national team. Proud of our journey.

I didn't make a speech in the locker room. The guys were disappointed, but it wasn't the right time. It would happen a little later, at dinner. Simple words, short sentences. I simply expressed my gratitude for everyone and for all those incredible years I experienced with the French team, and how proud I was to have shared that with them. I told everyone that all those years would be etched in my mind forever.

It was over. I had done what I had to do with the French team. I was 34. You have to know when to leave.

In the hotel room, I was obviously nostalgic as I packed up my stuff and closed my bag for the last time. The good times came flooding back. I forgot about the bad ones. What an experience! Being able to live it with Boris, one of my best friends, was incredible. When we were at INSEP, we never could have dreamed we'd be champions of Europe and the NBA together. Never.

The last night, in the hotel room, Bobo and I spent a lot of time talking. We were proud of our journey. The very next day I left for San Antonio. My baby was three weeks old. I couldn't wait to see my family again. As soon as I arrived in Texas, the Spurs had me get my foot checked out.

Blessed by the Gods

I regularly think about the French national team. Especially the good memories. Sometimes, when I was away with the NBA, I would treat myself and watch the 2013 semifinals against Spain again. Those were beautiful and important times in my life.

I went back to Coubertin in 2018 for a practice, and it was a strange feeling when I slipped my jersey back on and saw the team again. The French team was a big part of my life. I've never forgotten the criticism early in my career: "At any rate, you can't win an international competition with a point guard who scores, who is a 'ball dominant' point guard." It reminded me of my idol, Michael Jordan. People said he'd never win a title because it was impossible to win a title with the best scorer in the league. At the time, that drove him crazy. Those criticisms also drove me crazy. Why wouldn't we win with an aggressive point guard? That motivated me throughout the years. Jordan got used to it, and so did I. That's the sign of a great player. There were high expectations of me in every game I played with the French team. It was a huge responsibility. But I told myself I had the shoulders to carry it.

In the end, you can look at that long and beautiful experience in two ways. The Spurs would say that I came back tired from my seasons with the French team, and that I could have had an even greater career in the NBA if not for my international play. You could also say that incessantly chasing a title with the French national team fueled my desire to keep coming back, which was also beneficial for the Spurs.

I simply feel like I've been blessed by the gods. I don't regret anything. All those summers with the Blues were awesome. I'll always remember that magic moment when Lucien Legrand handed me my first blue jersey, the moment I put on the French national team jersey for the first time. It was in a U16 tournament in Bellegarde. We played against the Czech Republic. When he gave me the jersey, I looked at it and said to myself, "That's it. You're one of the best players in France. You're going to play for your country." Whether you're 14 or 35, that feeling is unparalleled.

I only kept the videos of the titles in my personal collection: the four NBA titles and the 2013 EuroBasket title. Of the four NBA titles, I don't even have films of all the games. Only the final win. On the other hand, for the

2013 EuroBasket, I kept both games: the semifinal against Spain and the final against Lithuania. In my 20-year career, I've only kept videos of those six games. That's it. Basically, the highest points of my career are contained in six DVDs. For example, I don't have the finals in Zadar with the French Juniors in 2000.

I also gave away all of my shoes except the ones I was wearing during the four NBA titles and the 2013 EuroBasket title. However, I've kept all my jerseys. All of them! They're in San Antonio. Even my first jersey in Fécamp when I was nine years old. The jerseys from clubs, drafts, the All-Star Game. I even have the one from the N1 All-Star Game when I was at INSEP. I have been N1 All-Star, Pro All-Star, and NBA All-Star. Not too shabby. I've kept one jersey from each NBA season, including the last one in Charlotte.

I wouldn't change anything about my time with the French national team. Each game, each phase, each experience had prepared us for being champions in 2013. I met great people in addition to my long-time friends Boris, Ronny, and Nico. A few players stand out.

One is Antoine Diot. I had a really special relationship with him. I loved playing with him, and I really liked when the coach had us play together on court. Antoine was a safe bet. You knew he was all-in for the team. He's so wholesome. He's really a good guy, and we had great times together.

In the beginning of my career, there was also Freddy Fauthoux. He was one of the veterans who took me under his wing. I admit that in the beginning, before I knew him, I had a negative opinion about him. I would tell myself, "That guy must be a dick." In my opinion, at the time, the guys from Pau were so annoying. Freddy came across as a pain in the ass who was booed in every arena. In fact, he was completely the opposite when I got to know him. He's really an endearing person. I really liked him, and when we won the bronze medal in 2005, I was sincerely happy to be able to win it with him.

I also had a good relationship with my coaches on the French team. Things were really great with Alain Weisz, and I had a great relationship with Claude Bergeaud. I liked him a lot. He had a different way of thinking about things. Obviously, I'll always have a special relationship with Vincent Collet, because we won a title together and we were together for more than seven years. It was short-lived with Michel Gomez—only about six weeks during the qualifiers—so I didn't really have a chance to develop a special relationship with him.

When I closed that bag for the last time in my hotel room in Rio, I took so many good times and good memories with me. There was also the trip to Croatia in 2000 with the U18 team. I was 18, and an all-expenses paid trip to the beach was an overindulgence to me. Bobo and I had a lot of fun. The party after winning the title was memorable. Bobo got really sick. We had to carry him, put him in a shopping cart, and push him all the way back to the hotel.

At the other end of the spectrum, on the day of the 2013 EuroBasket final, Boris and I sat in our hotel room and reminisced, and then took a nap. It was a nostalgic time, and we talked about how far we had come and how we were finally going to make it. There were so many moments in between. There were also all those great nights in our basecamp at Villa Navarre in Pau. It was our cocoon, and we were happy there. The titleholders had their own rooms. I was happy when Axelle would come to see me.

In terms of structure, reception, and comfort, Boris and I helped the French national team evolve. We mirrored the NBA's framework. We brought the French team's physical therapists to San Antonio so that they could observe the Spurs' system. We brought an osteopath on staff. We managed to sometimes travel by private jet in order to make recovery easier. We managed to get a one-person-per-room change during training camps in France.

With the NBA as our model, Bobo and I kind of changed the code of conduct in France. For example, we were able to get some optional dinners authorized for players who wanted to go eat at a restaurant. It wasn't easy to gain acceptance for that idea, because at the time, the French national team tradition was to eat all meals together. We also established an optional breakfast for those who wanted to sleep a little longer. We started that with Joakim Noah. He didn't eat too many breakfasts with us in 2011. It's good that we were able to change those things.

With the referees, it turned out to be a long road. We had to get to know them and learn their first names. By 2011 I had earned their respect, but it had taken me almost 10 years. I might have been an NBA All-Star, but when I got to Europe, I was basically a rookie. But I had to go through that. I was told that the road would be long and complicated on the French national team. But from the start, I never gave up, and it became a long and beautiful love story. Today, when I look back on what we did, I'm proud of what we accomplished.

CHAPTER FOUR

My Life
in Business

Ever since I was little, I wanted to be part of the business world. My parents were not part of that world, and I had zero connections. But it was one of my dreams.

One night when I was 14 or 15, during my time on the U18 French team, my friend Gaëtan Mullers and I were talking before going to bed. I told him, "I want to go to the NBA, participate in the basketball camps, and when I'm retired, we'll buy a club!"

"Okay, we'll do it!" he said.

Gaëtan liked to say that those were our "three dreams." I knew early on that it was something I wanted to sink my teeth into. Ronny Turiaf often laughed about it. At the time, I played *FIFA Manager* a lot. Ronny would say, "Are you preparing for your post-career or what?" Managing clubs, budgets, purchases, trading players, etc. I loved that game. Years later when I bought ASVEL, Ronny sent me this message, as a nod to my *FIFA Manager* days: "Okay, you've fulfilled your dream. You're going to be able to play manager for real now."

Early on, I paid close attention to the business of the game. I was aware of my evolving public image. In 2003, when I became the first French NBA champion and offers were coming out of the woodwork, I realized that I was blowing up in France. I didn't immediately throw myself into business, but I understood that I was becoming kind of an ambassador of French basketball. I wanted to rise to the challenge. With the advice of my mother, I started my foundation, the Par Coeur Gala, and I set up basketball camps.

I really have my mother to thank for my first foray into the business side of basketball. She's the one that really pushed for us to help the youth that don't have the same opportunities I had. She made me aware of that early on, and after spending a little time in hospitals, I couldn't help but be touched by and sure of the importance of such a decision.

The Par Coeur Gala is an opportunity to change peoples' lives a little. We manage to raise between 200,000 and 250,000 euros per year, and we make donations to different organizations every year. I have also served as an ambassador for the Make-A-Wish Foundation for over 10 years. Personally, I donate the same amount to different organizations in San Antonio. I'm also a member of the board of directors of the San Antonio Zoo, to which I also provide financial assistance to protect certain animal species.

My passion for basketball eventually inspired me to establish and run basketball camps. I really enjoyed it. In general, a professional athlete who has a camp only goes there once or twice a week, stays for two hours, and that's it. In the beginning, in Fécamp, my brothers and I would stay for two out of the three weeks the camp was open, and I was with the kids from 9:00 AM until midnight. Any kid who has gone to one of my camps would say it was incredible. The idea is that it's a family-like atmosphere, and the camp is close-knit. I know the names of all the kids. They can come talk to me whenever they want. I take part in the exercises and play one-on-one games all day. Even today, the camps last for two weeks and I stay for five for six days. Given everything else I have going on, I can't stay as long as I did before. In 2018, we closed the camp in Fécamp. We decided to focus on the camp in Lyon, the Academy, and the camp in Rosey, Switzerland. I can't be everywhere, and if I can't have a quality camp, I would rather close it. It's important for me now to be in Lyon, and it's easier for me to be onsite, all while managing my businesses, in particular, ASVEL.

Conscious of My Image

Around the same time I launched my foundation in 2003, I had to sort through all of the sponsorship offers that were pouring in. They were considerable sources of revenue, but I didn't want to commit to just anything. I carefully chose the advertising campaigns I would do.

Having close control of my image was important to me. In that regard, I was inspired by my idol, Michael Jordan, who had successfully created an almost perfect image throughout his career. At the time, basketball didn't carry much weight in France. I wanted to move it out of the purely athletic domain and make it a little more mainstream and alluring.

I obviously couldn't do that alone. So I chose a team to advise me and surrounded myself with them. Morgan Menahem oversaw marketing and sponsorship contracts, and Ludo Longuet was my press agent. The idea was to convey a good personal image, of course, but also to *sell* French basketball. The Federation quickly jumped on board so that they could talk about their sport and help it evolve in France.

My first big contract was Nike. That came well before my first NBA title. I was 17 and playing for PSG. I had signed a four-year contract. At the time, I was supposed to earn 100,000 to 150,000 euros per year with Nike. When I became an NBA champion in 2003, the timing was perfect. My first contract was almost over, and I signed a new, bigger contract with them: eight years at 1.5 million euros per year. That's when everything really took off.

A Tour de France of Basketball

The first time I truly realized the impact I was having on French basketball was in the summer of 2002, when I came back to France after my first season in the NBA. With Nike, we held my first basketball camp at La Défense.

It was madness. We had set up a court in the square of La Défense and brought in a lot of NBA players: Bruce Bowen, Malik Rose, and Cuttino Mobley, just to name a few. We held a gala game with Yannick Noah, Gad Elmaleh, Marie-José Pérec, and several others. The square was packed. I watched it all, a little astounded, and said to myself, "These people have come to see me."

That day I realized I really needed to surround myself with the right people and do things the right way. The 2003 NBA title in my second year, when I averaged 16 points per game as Tim Duncan's lieutenant with the Spurs, really set everything in motion.

After that, my career was on a roll. In 2003, I signed with Bollé sunglasses, Kinder, and Bouygues Telecom. Then I did commercials for Frosties that were linked to my basketball camps. I quickly realized that business is a big nonstop machine.

At the time, with Bouygues, we did basketball camps and toured all around France. I went everywhere with my brothers. We laugh when we talk about it now. It was the beginning of my career. We were living like musicians, like rock stars. We changed cities every morning and traveled by train. We were exhausted. We would get to a city, play three-on-three, party at night, and then the next morning, dead tired, we would take another train to do it all over again in another city. We played and went out at night. It was awesome. I was 21 years old. I traveled to all the cities in France. I was an NBA champion, and wherever we went it was packed. I did that for three summers, 2003, 2004, and 2005. Each tour lasted for about two weeks, and we went to around a dozen cities each time.

My sponsorship choices were always influenced by the products I had consumed throughout my life. For example, I never would have repped Coca-Cola because I didn't drink it. On the other hand, Powerade was popular in the NBA and I drank it. I wanted my sponsorships to reflect me, to be me. When I was little, before going to school, I would eat Frosties for breakfast. It made sense that they would come along for the ride. I loved Nutella, so Kinder made sense.

When you play 5,000 miles from France, it's not easy to do business there, and my schedule was very tight. As soon as the NBA season was over, which was in the end of June during the seasons when we went to the Finals, and before the French team got together, I generally had two or three weeks to make my appearances and do my performances and camps. I didn't take a vacation, and after, I immediately left for the French national team's training camp.

Learning the Business

I find business fascinating. I'm part of the first generation of athletes who can financially influence their own sport. It's not for everyone, though. You're either made for it or not. Some players aren't interested in it at all. You have to realize that managing a club is work. It's not like a training session where you spend an hour or two on the court, and then do what you want the rest of the day.

It would start at 8:00 AM: all-day meetings, debriefings, paying attention to details. It's an entire day's work. Most lose their concentration after 45 minutes in a meeting. The business world doesn't permit that. But I don't feel like I'm working when I schedule a board meeting at 8:00 AM or a meeting in my office with my stockholders. I get there at 8:00, and I'm happy; we delve into the numbers, we probe, we analyze fan feedback, discuss merchandising, how to sell various products, and whether or not we should raise or lower prices.

I'm interested in it because I'm involved in all areas. I've read books and spent time listening to people. I've always tried to surround myself with the right people. It started with my passion, my vision, and my ability to unite people on the court. For all the areas I was unfamiliar with, I learned about them.

I was lucky to come across people who were willing to teach me. I often bombarded my financial adviser, Stéphane Oberer, with questions. I read all the books that he recommended on finance. I won't pretend to be a legal expert, but I learned a lot through working with my lawyer, Didier Domat. I also loved Magic Johnson's *32 Ways to Be a Champion in Business* and took every word to heart. Drawing inspiration from the experiences of those who have succeeded is important. When I was traveling, it was the kind of book I would have on my nightstand in the hotel room. I stopped playing video games around the age of 22 or 23. I started reading more instead, preparing myself for that other world. I always had those books with me. At some point, educating oneself is paramount.

When I met Stéphane Oberer, he immediately told me, "You're 22 years old, but you talk like you're 30." I didn't know anything about finance, but I asked him to teach me, to educate me. Our meetings would last for two hours. There was a bottle of water on my dining room table for each guest. I knew it was going to take a while.

I wanted to learn, I wanted to know everything. I refused to give away $10 million just like that, to be thrown to the wind. I wanted to know the strategy, why we were investing in certain things, and what the end goal was.

I would guess that 95 percent of athletes trust third parties with their money, depend on them fully, and don't follow up on where their money goes. That's why a lot of them get swindled and lose large sums in investments. I always watched where my money was going and participated in the planning. Today, I make the decisions almost exclusively on my own.

I Consider Myself a Machine

At the very beginning of my business training, when I was still playing, a business day at my house in San Antonio started at 6:00 or 7:00 AM. Around 10:00 AM, I would leave for practice. Afterward, I would come home, have a little lunch, and then, in the afternoon, we would talk and put the different situations and scenarios into practice.

My financial and legal advisers usually stayed there for a week so that I could learn from them. It was a little like a seminar. I was starting from scratch. I didn't know how to read or present a budget. Today, I've mastered all of that. I have learned how to make decisions, look at a situation clearly, and bring people together. I think that's my biggest strength: inspiring people and setting a good example. I don't keep track of my time. I don't think that just because my name is Tony Parker, I don't need to show up prepared and on time for a business meeting.

Even when I was playing, I never felt like I was doing too much or was too busy. I felt like a machine. It was fascinating. For example, during the French championship finals in June of 2019, I was with the team in Monaco, the day after Game 4, which we had just lost. In the morning, at the hotel, we had a meeting about club finances from 9:00 AM to 1:00 PM, before leaving the area. At 2:00 we got on the plane, and at 4:00 we landed in Rouen, where the French women's team was playing a practice game for the EuroBasket. We immediately went to the arena. I said hi to everyone, greeted my ASVEL players, Marine Johannès and Marième Badiane, and we talked for a few minutes. The game started at 6:30 PM. We stayed for the first half then rushed to the Havre for the French women's football World Cup game. We got there 45 minutes before the game. I saw Noël Le Graët, president of the French Football Federation (FFF), and Jean-Michel Aulas, the owner of Olympique Lyonnais, which is a successful French soccer club. We watched the game. They won, and then we drove back to Rouen. We got there at 1:30 in the morning, slept a little, and the next day we raced over to my old middle school for the Paris 2024 event. There had been some improvements, but I still recognized it. The main doors were still burgundy, and I even walked around my classroom. I spent two hours there with the kids, and at 11:00 AM, we drove back to Paris.

In the car, when we finally had a few minutes to breathe, I looked at the people who were with me, and I said cheerfully, "Those two days in Normandy were great!" Everyone burst out laughing. It hadn't even been 24 hours, and we had crossed France from Monaco to Rouen. We hadn't stopped moving. But I found it fascinating. My friends and I call it "the fast life." That's how it is with me: life in the fast lane.

Of course, I could rest more and take more vacations. But for me, it's no secret. When we did the hat trick with ASVEL (girls' and boys' champion titles and a boys' French Cup in 2019), I didn't say, "Wow! What a great season! How crazy!" Yes, it was crazy. I'm proud of what we did. But there was also part of me that said, "I deserve it."

I work so hard to make sure everyone is okay, and that the players are healthy and ready to play. Whether it's athletic or administrative, we get results because of all that work. If you want to make history, you have to do the work. That's how I motivate my teams. When the ASVEL boys became champions, we hadn't even celebrated the win when I said to them in the locker room, "That's good, but now the goal is to create a dynasty. We have to try to dominate." That's how I grew up with the Spurs. When we won three titles in five years, we didn't want to settle for that. We wanted to dominate, mark our territory, and make history.

It's too easy to rest on your laurels, to win a title and then take it easy. I could have done that in 2016, when we won the title after my second year as president of ASVEL. I could have said to myself, "It's good. It's going to be fine." On the contrary, it gave me even more motivation to win more titles. Now, after two titles in four years, I only have one word in mind: dynasty. That's how you make history.

I'm Not an Easy-Going Boss

I like to be in control. I like knowing all the details. In August of 2019, I invited the girls from ASVEL to spend one week at my house in San Antonio. I was the one who set up the timing for the week, who decided what we were going to do each day, and who chose each restaurant.

I want to be a hands-on father. I drop my boys off at school every morning. But I'm not the type of guy to stay at home and spend all my time with my kids. However, I want to make sure they know I'm there for them.

Money was never an incentive to get into business. I made my fortune with the NBA. I never wanted money or potential earnings to influence my choices in business. When you take over a club like ASVEL, you're not doing it for the money. Sometimes, people don't understand. I have a lot of investments and businesses that are not necessarily visible. I have several million dollars out there. They're calculated risks. I hope they take off one day so that I can invest in even more passion projects, like the one I have with both ASVEL clubs. Although I like for my investments to be profitable, I especially want them to be protected, particularly on behalf of the stockholders who trust me with their money. In that regard, it's clear that our relationship with Jean-Michel Aulas and Olympique Lyonnais (OL) protects those investments. With OL as a partner, all of our investments are now safe.

I don't think I'm a tough boss, simply a demanding one. I don't keep track of my hours, and I expect my partners to work as hard as I do. I don't get angry, but sometimes I resort to motivating speeches. Since I can choose who I'm going to work with, and I want to be sure things don't get out of control, I'm not an easy-going boss. I'm commanding, but I delegate. My employees must have freedom. Yes, I'm stern about certain things, but at the same time I trust them. I study people before giving them leeway.

When Didier Domat came to my house for the first time, I barely spoke to him for two days, and he wondered what he was doing there. Before he became my lawyer, I needed to figure out his character traits and see how he would react in certain situations. I needed to see if he would get angry, take things further, or stay calm. I wanted to test him.

I've studied and talked to most of my employees. There are only a few exceptions. For the first time last year, an employee started at the Academy, and I hadn't talked with him yet. We were expanding too quickly, and there just wasn't time for me to get to know him first. But I make it a priority to know who is working for me. At ASVEL alone, between the club and the Academy, and everything that happens with the club, there are around 70 employees, and I've gotten to know all of them.

I've never been afraid to take risks. With business, you have to take some from time to time. Today, I'm no longer looking for notoriety or the classic sponsorship image like I did at the beginning of my career. I only have four sponsorships: Tissot, Peak, Teisseire, and Puressentiel. I don't need to be seen. I still get offers for commercials and things like that. But it's no longer a priority. I think we did good work throughout the years. We were consistent. When I retired and gauged the impact I made on French sports as a whole, it's heartwarming. I don't regret any of my past sponsorships. They've all made sense for me.

Villard-de-Lans

Today, I do so much business—in sports, cinema, and other domains—that I make decisions based on how the opportunity feels to me. It's a matter of whether or not I like a project or an idea.

Take Villard-de-Lans, for example. It was completely unplanned. I never would have thought I'd buy a ski resort. Then one of my sponsors from the women's club brought me the project. The town council didn't want someone from outside the country to buy the operating rights. They thought it would be better for the management of the resort to stay in France.

I thought about it, studied the collaborations we could create, and considered the logistics for a global project with ASVEL. I decided that it would allow us to expand our market. We would need to fill our new 10,000-seat arena in a few years. I started to have some ideas: plan a gala game in Grenoble to raise awareness and reach a new audience. We could take our preseason training for both teams to Villard-de-Lans so that the club could be the star of the Rhône-Alpes region. The project slowly started to become feasible and interesting. "Come on, let's do it!" I decided.

I visited Villard-de-Lans for the first time with Maria-Sophie Obama, the vice president of the women's ASVEL Lyon, in the summer of 2018. We took a chopper and fell for the place immediately. In business, just like in a lot of other areas of life, decisions are often a matter of intuition.

You either see yourself doing it or you don't. We had a great feeling about it.

Afterward, we looked at the numbers to see if it could be an attractive business opportunity. Because the resort spanned two cities, I met with both mayors, from Villard and Corrençon-en-Vercors. I was introduced to the owners of the operation, two brothers who were 92 and 94 years old, respectively, and then a few other people from the resort. I had a good feeling about the project. After a single day, I knew that if the price matched my offer, I was going to buy it. It cost $9 million for the winter and summer operations. As is often the case, I have the majority of shares in the project, along with other shareholders, including Marie-Sophie Obama, Nicolas Batum, and some people from Villard, as well as the sponsor who brought me the deal.

The project could seem surprising, given the fact that there is no direct connection to basketball. Besides, I had never gone skiing. But you have to know how to diversify.

The same is true for my production company. I didn't think I would invest in cinema, and then I had the opportunity to go to Broadway with *Mean Girls*, the musical adaptation of the *Mean Girls* movie. My show was the hottest in New York. I attended the Tony awards, yet another new experience filled with new encounters. Another opportunity, a new door opens, you meet new people, and your circle gets bigger. That's how it works.

That's how I looked at investing in the ski resort. It enabled me to meet Martin Fourcade and to discover a new world. I intend to have a business that works. The goal isn't solely to make money. I want to have a good project that the people associated with the resort will be proud of. I want the resort to retain the village atmosphere and family-oriented feel.

When I went back to France in the spring of 2019, all people could talk about was Villard. During her show, *Au Tableau!,* Mélissa Theuriau told me, "I grew up in Villard. It was my childhood resort." I didn't think it would make such an impact. On the night of June 10, 2019, the day I announced my retirement from sports, I went to the Maroon 5 concert. People talked more about Villard than my retirement. Axelle has skied for years, and my kids went skiing for the first time in Aspen in the winter of 2018. My big debut on the slopes was during the winter of 2019. I really want to spend time there, be it summer or winter.

Now, it has to be love at first sight since I already have a lot of business ventures. But I won't rule anything out.

ASVEL, My New Challenge

With ASVEL, I had the opportunity to make history once more despite my playing career being over. It was really exciting.

In the beginning, I wanted to do something in Paris. I had played there for two years, and it seemed logical for me to invest in my former club. I looked into it with Mark Fleisher, my agent and potential business partner at the time, but I couldn't see myself doing it. Besides, the mayor and the president of the region didn't look favorably on an American taking over the club.

So I decided to investigate other clubs. I made it known that I wanted to invest and asked managers to introduce me to their clubs. Four delegations, along with their mayors, came to San Antonio in 2008: Lille, Montpellier, ASVEL, and Marseille. After the presentations, I chose ASVEL. Being a big city and economic area, I told myself it would be possible to increase the budget and develop something really great. I also liked Gilles Moretton's speech. He was a former tennis player and the current owner of the club. He told me he couldn't keep the job forever. If I came on board, he could step down.

So in 2009, I became a minority shareholder of ASVEL. I took 10 percent for 500,000 euros. In 2012, I took on another 10 percent. The initial strategy was to take over the club after I retired from sports. But I saw that the sponsors hesitated to come on board because I wasn't the president. It would happen much more quickly if I were, and so in 2014, I decided to take control of the club. There were a lot of negotiations. It took close to two years.

I managed to buy the club for 2 million euros, although it was worth 5 million. I had been with the club since 2009, and I knew exactly how much money it lost every year and how much the shareholders had to put back into it during that time. So when the negotiations began, I immediately said I wasn't going to buy a club for 5 million euros that was losing money and would require putting some back in every year. They had started with 5 million, then 4, then 3.5. I didn't change my price and made them understand that it was better to get 2 million than nothing at all. I would take on all the responsibilities. All they would have to do was reinvest and they could remain shareholders with me in the new organizational chart.

Jacques Gaillard, Roland Tchénio, and Michel Garcia were notable shareholders and real fans of the club. I said to the three of them, "You can stay on board with me. I won't ask you for a single penny." In the end, they accepted.

Of course, Gilles Moretton was disappointed. When you spend 13 years with a club, it must be difficult to give it up. He knew he would step down one day, but he thought he would do it five or six years later. No doubt it must have been a bit brutal for him, but honestly, he remained agreeable throughout the process.

I brought in Bruno Rousset and two former NBA players, Corey Maggette and Michael Finley. When I took over the club, I took on everything. In my second season, we won the 2016 champion of France title. Then everything took off. Nicolas Batum came on board in 2017. He became a shareholder in both the men's and women's clubs. In five years, we had two championship titles, a championship trophy, and a French Cup, and we achieved two capital increases.

But it wasn't always so easy. At first, the three notable shareholders didn't want to participate in the capital increase, because they didn't believe in the women's Lyon ASVEL. I said to them, "It's men's and women's, or nothing." They refused. So Nico and I took on the capital increase together, and the move diluted their shares.

I didn't take it personally. I respected their decision. It gave me motivation. I knew that the women's side was risky, especially since the women's Lyon club was riddled with debt. It was quite a long shot, but I wanted to prove that the overall project of uniting the women's and men's clubs was a good idea and would make the club worth more. It's incredible what we were able to create in two years with the women's club.

Today, when they see how the club has evolved, those shareholders regret their initial stance. When we became champions of France with the women's club in May 2019, they were the first to say, "Well done!" In fact, to protect their shares from becoming further diluted, they backed the next capital increase. Today, the shareholders are happy. They're on board, they believe in the overall project, and they feel secure with the addition of OL to the capital. In five years, the estimated value of the club went from 5 to 15 million euros.

I'm proud of what we've accomplished over the last five years. For the men's finals, we could have had 12,000 people, and for the women's finals, I'm sure we could have filled the Astroballe.

I had a passion. I had a vision. I was motivated, and seeing how everyone is on board today makes me really happy. Buying ASVEL was my first major project. I knew that I could lose all my investment. I was aware of the risk, because French basketball is not the NBA. There were a lot of uncertainties with the club, the arena, the EuroLeague, the partners, and the Academy. Who was going to follow me?

I took risks in choosing people too. I made 33-year-old Gaëtan Muller president of ASVEL. It drew tons of criticism: "Parker took over the oldest club in France and put his buddy in charge." I wouldn't choose a friend just because he was my friend. I made the decision because I knew Gaëtan was able to handle it, and I knew he would excel. I also heard, "They don't know what they're doing. They've never managed a budget. They've never signed a big deal." All of that was true, but I wanted to tell them, "Give me a chance. It's up to us to prove it to you." Five years later, you can see the path the club took. Gaëtan, Marie-Sophie, and I are a killer team. Both of them work really hard, and their contribution to the club's success is enormous.

The double in 2019 was almost a validation of all the work we did over five years. France had lost the EuroLeague, and we brought the EuroLeague to France. It was a hell of a job to wear them down. When I approached Jordi Bertomeu, the president of the EuroLeague, he no longer wanted to hear anything about France. He was fed up. That was the tone of our first conversations. We had to restore France's image, ASVEL's image. Of course, my name being Tony Parker helped. In the beginning, it's leverage for everything. It does help open doors and bend ears. But I still have to prove myself and show that there is something behind the name. My name might be Tony Parker, but if my project sucks, I don't work hard, or I sit still and think it will come on its own, I know I won't get very far. In 2019, I had two champion titles, the EuroLeague, and the deal with OL, which is the only one of its kind in French sports. So, yes, for me, that validated all the work we had accomplished in five years.

I put 7 million euros of my own money into the ASVEL project. It's a lot of money. It made me laugh when people said, "Yeah, it's easy. He's paying." But I'm not sorry. I don't see other athletes doing that. A lot of them don't want to spend money like that and risk losing it. It's not that easy. In order to spend 7 million, I needed to earn 14 million because of the taxes. It's a ton of money, and it's not coming from my business. It's my own money. It's a commitment in my own name. It's the same for Nicolas Batum. We both took huge risks. People need to understand that.

I talked with people who were a lot richer than I was to try to convince them to help me with the project. They told me that they weren't interested in sports. With their money, they could change the lives of millions of people, but they weren't interested. I know a lot of people who sit on their money and do nothing with it. Others only want to invest if they're sure to earn it back. I want people to understand that. I took risks. I bought the club. I built the Academy. I don't invest my money in businesses that are certainly not going to pay off.

A Tough Business

Managing a club also means making difficult decisions. Letting Pierre Vincent go from his position as coach in November of 2014 was the most difficult one I've had to make since I started managing the club. I really liked him. He had a huge influence on my career, and he's a good coach. It was hard for him. He had been on good terms with the club but has since broken off all ties. Today, we no longer have a relationship. That's my only regret. We might again someday. But I don't regret my decision—it was the right thing to do.

I tell everyone who works with me, and all of my friends, "Maybe one day I'll have to decide to let you go." I will always do what I think is right for the club. That doesn't mean I'll always be right. Given the results we were getting at the time with Pierre Vincent, combined with the shareholders' doubts, and the fact that the players had also lost confidence in him, it was impossible to keep him on board.

I called him and explained the situation. On the phone, I immediately sensed that it affected him deeply. But he was fair. He didn't sue the club, unlike JD Jackson, who was fired in January of 2018. He told me everything was okay and then sued me afterward. I will always be grateful to JD. We won our first title under his coaching. But afterward, we could tell he wouldn't be the one to take us to the next level. I know I was right. In 2019, we won the double with practically the same team, except for two players. That proved that I was right. That's how it is with business. I'm not one to hold a grudge. We'll settle what we have to settle with lawyers. That's life.

When my brother TJ took over after JD Jackson and finished the season, does anyone think it was easy for me to tell him that he had to go back to being assistant coach the following season? Those are decisions that need to be made, and I take responsibility for them. I'm the one who decides to work with family and friends when they're competent and can do the job. I can't allow emotions to take control. There is a time for family and friends and a time for business. I'm not going to jeopardize all of my investments and those of the shareholders who believe in me simply because I want to keep a friend or family member on my staff.

Today, I think my brother is ready. He has the ability and enough experience to carry the team forward. Back then, he couldn't deal with the looming deadlines. It wasn't the right time for him. Maybe I was being overprotective, but he understood my decision. His time will come, and I'll give him his chance. You can bet on that. He learned from Pierre Vincent. He learned from JD Jackson. And he learned from Zvezdan Mitrovic. As a player and assistant coach, my brother has over 10 trophies. He knows the French championships

BEYOND ALL OF MY DREAMS

by heart. He is ready. Logically, he'll be the one to take over. At any rate, that's what I'm preparing him for.

All Ego?

A sports club business is still built around people, and it's my job to manage everyone's feelings. You can't be a good leader without handling everyone's egos and without understanding everyone's problems. I take a lot of time to get to know who my players are. I get to know their families. The women from ASVEL are like my daughters. I don't have any daughters in my house, and I always say that the women's team are my "little girls." I spend a lot of time on the phone with them, and we really have a special relationship. I also have a real relationship with the boys, but it's not as profound. Whereas I talk on the phone four or five times per month on average with a female player, I only talk once a month with the men.

I'm definitely a president who is close to his players. It's no coincidence that Charles Kahudi signed a five-year contract with us. If Edwin Jackson came back to ASVEL, it's because we're really close. Same with the American players. I always try to stay in touch. I don't have to do that. We're almost the same age and are into the same things. When we celebrated the women's title in spring of 2019, I danced with them. They told me they never had a president who danced with them, drank right from the bottle, or took shots with them. Marie-Sophie and I actually are the ones who get the party started. In general, a president is 20 or 30 years older than they are. It strengthens the human bond that exists in the club.

I'm so in tune with my players' well-being that managing remotely has never been a problem. Take Alysha Clark, for example. I called her in January of 2018 to ask her to sign with my club. I knew a little about her. She had played in San Antonio with the WNBA, but I had never met her. She signed with us. The season came to an end, and we lost in the semifinals. Then the new season started, and I still hadn't met Alysha. We talked to each other on the phone several times per month and had some good laughs. The first time we met face-to-face was on May 6, 2019, the morning of Game 1 of the finals, even though she had been with us for a year and a half by then. We gave each other a big hug as if we knew each other, but it was the first time I had met her in person. We had talked so many times throughout the season that, in the end, it was as if we had been hanging out every day.

That's what's impressive, the bond I've managed to create despite my not always being present in Lyon. It's going to be awesome now that I'm going to be there more often. It'll be nice to go there every six weeks and be there for the big games: The Leaders Cup, the big EuroLeague games. I will be able to take a few trips with the team.

Where Does Basketball Fit In?

The first time I had control over the athletics at ASVEL was during the 2011–12 season. I even played with the team. Gilles Moretton made the financial and budgetary decisions, and I had to live with it, but I chose the players, the coach, and even the physical therapist.

At the time, I was still learning. I didn't really know what direction to go. I had invested a million euros and owned 20 percent of the club. If I didn't like it, I would sell it. Though the athletic season was not a success, I never thought I was bad at the job.

The season was a little short. There was an NBA lockout that year, so Ronny Turiaf and I played with ASVEL for two months. We started out well, and the club qualified for the EuroCup Top 16. When we went back to the NBA, the ASVEL players no longer knew their roles. The club finished 10th that season and didn't make the playoffs. It was a strange season. Pierre Vincent and I built the team. He was also a novice when it came to coaching the boys, and it was a learning process for both of us. We were both rookies, and we did the best we could with what we had.

The following year we had a real season. We finished third in the regular season and were in the championship and French Cup semifinals—with the same budget from the previous season. It was already a huge improvement.

Starting in 2014, when I became president and seriously invested, we began forming substantial teams. We lost the first round of the playoffs against Le Mans. Nico Batum was at the ASVEL game. At the time, he was involved with the club management in the MSB project. That's when we had our first talks. Nico wasn't really happy with Le Mans. He didn't feel like he was part of a family. There were a lot of older players, and he was unhappy there. When he saw my team, which was young and always joking around with Gaëtan, Yohann Sangaré, and Alexis Lefebvre, he told me he would like to come to ASVEL.

At first, I didn't really think he was serious. I thought he wanted to do his own thing with Le Mans. But we talked about it again in the summer on the French national team, and then again in 2016. After the championship, I considered taking over the women's club, and I discussed it with Nico. I told him it would be perfect if he came on board. We needed several people to join forces in order to form a respectable EuroLeague club. His eyes lit up. I won him over, and he gave in. He told Le Mans he was leaving, and he's happy with us now. He is completely in his element. He manages the athletics and the training center. He's got the touch. He was the one who pushed for Mantas Kalnietis. He made his mark.

During the 2018–19 season, there were five of us on the recruiting team: Gaëtan, Yoyo Sangaré, Nico, the coach, and me. Everyone pushes for their favorite players and gets teased when the rookies have a bad game. But if a recruit is a success or a failure, we all take responsibility. It's a collective decision.

David Lighty and John Roberson are good examples. I didn't think John Roberson would party every night in clubs and go off the rails. Conversely, David Lighty is probably going to stay with us for seven years. There was never a problem. He's never missed one practice. Recruiting isn't an exact science. Our club has its own philosophy. We like to give out long contracts. Sometimes we're going to come across a John Roberson. We had signed him for two years. It didn't work out. We agreed on a deal, it cost us a little money to remove him, but that's how it is, and we dealt with it. It has worked nicely since I've taken over the club. We've won titles, and we've bonded with the fans. They can relate to a team that has an identity and that keeps its players. That's rare in France. All of the Pro A clubs completely change their team every year. Now Jean-Michel Aulas of OL will have a say in the recruiting process.

The Relationship with OL

Obviously, OL partnering with ASVEL in June 2019 was a key date in the history of our club. I first met Jean-Michel Aulas in 2006. He had come for an EA Sports event. We quickly hit it off. When I joined ASVEL in 2009, he attended the Par Coeur Gala dinner in support of my foundation. He took a few years to observe the club and to see what I was going to do with it. In 2016, when we were champions, he was one of the first people to send me a congratulatory text. When the opportunity for a collaboration presented itself, everything happened really quickly.

Jean-Michel is 30 years older than I am. Our relationship proves you never know who you'll get along with. There are people my age that I don't click with at all. It's a matter of instinct. I've always liked people who succeed. It's inspiring. Jean-Michel and I have the same work ethic. He's a machine, too, a tornado. We're on the same wavelength during meetings. But when I first met him, we didn't talk about business at all. It was really a friendly meeting, and there was mutual respect.

I never imagined that OL would invest in ASVEL. He was actually the one who brought it up, in December 2018. It never would have occurred to me to approach OL as an investor, but one day Jean-Michel called me.

"Tony, I think working together could be a good thing."

I was taken aback but obviously enthusiastic. I had to ask him to repeat himself.

It was an incredible opportunity for us, even if I wasn't necessarily looking for other shareholders. Nico and I had invested our own money, and we managed to keep it that way. But having OL as a partner was like having a secret weapon.

We started discussing it and looking at how we could collaborate. It had to be a give-and-take deal. I wanted to offer OL something too. And so we arrived at a deal. I think he realized just what a global force the NBA was. OL is backed by both Chinese and American investment funds, two countries that love basketball. I think that's how the idea started in his mind.

Later there was the arena opportunity. Jean-Michel Aulas is an entrepreneur. He's always looking for ways to raise OL's profile. If I were the president of a soccer club, I'd do the same thing. Basketball and soccer are very closely related. Pro soccer players often attend NBA games: Thierry Henry, Griezmann, Zizou, Mbappé, who was at Golden State when they were in the NBA Finals. It makes a lot of sense. For our women's finals, OL's women's soccer players were in the arena. Barça took on Pau Gasol as ambassador. Jean-Michel Aulas must have told himself that having Tony Parker as

OL's ambassador could make sense. He's really involved in the ASVEL project. He's not just there to provide money.

In the summer of 2019, we tried to bring Monaco's point guard, Dee Bost, on board. Jean-Michel's eyes lit up and he asked me, "Is Dee Bost the point guard that killed us in Games 3 and 4?"

"Yes, the very same."

He was ready to offer 200,000 euros more to get Bost on our team. Jean-Michel put a lot of money into ASVEL, 18 million in total. It makes sense that he would participate in building out the team. I wanted him to be part of the recruitment team.

Soccer brings in more money than basketball. As the men's ASVEL partner, OL invests 2.5 million euros per year. They could probably invest more, but I don't want to take advantage of the partnership. A private partner has never come on board and poured 2.5 million euros per year over five years into any French basketball club. Only soccer can do that. LDLC invests 1.1 million each year, which is already huge. The other big clubs, like Strasbourg and Le Mans, probably get around 300,000 or 400,000 euros a year from their investors.

My work with Jean-Michel is an open book. He now knows very well that Nico and I will no longer invest the millions that we did in previous years. I'm now focused on the Academy. It has to start off well, and there will be other investments to be made. I wasn't going to inject money into it every year. That wasn't the goal. Nico and I, for the 2019–20 season, reinvested 500,000 each, but only for the women's team.

OL's investment in ASVEL's capital was not a takeover. That's not in the cards. I count on keeping the club for a long time. With the partners' agreement, I have to remain president for at least another five years. For now, I'm fully devoted to the club, and I want to stay there. I can't say what will happen in 10 years, but I know that over the next five years, we're going to keep developing the club. We're going to build a new stadium. I hope we'll have the EuroLeague for life.

I don't know where Jean-Michel will be in five years. He'll be 75. I like thinking about things in five-year increments. Every five years I'll take stock of where we are and decide what happens next. At 25 percent, OL is already the club's second-biggest shareholder. Will Jean-Michel want to ramp things up? We'll see. I'm going to work hand in hand with OL. For now, he doesn't really need to take on any more. I own 55 percent, Nico owns 15 percent, and the other 5 percent is spread out. What I know for sure is that Nico and OL will be involved in every future decision. But I'm okay with that. OL can only help us advance.

In my opinion, Jean-Michel is by far the best sports club president from the last 30 years. OL is a war machine. They're listed on the stock market, and last year, they made 300 million euros in turnover. We have so much to learn from them. Up until now, Gaëtan and I have done what we can to increase the club's wealth to 15 million. The next step is with OL, by pooling partners together, particularly in the women's sector, where OL dominates European soccer.

I Try to Inspire People

When they joined ASVEL, Jean-Michel and his right-hand man, Thierry Sauvage, immediately participated in their first board of directors meeting. It was very symbolic and moving to see OL at the same table as Marc Lefebvre, president of ASVEL in the 1990s. For me, Marc's opinion is very important. He's part of the club's history. There are now nine of us on the board of directors, six from ASVEL and three from OL. There are 10 members in the club's ownership.

What I like most about managing a club is inspiring people. Having a vision, generating motivation, setting goals, and bringing everyone together. I love that. Alexis Lefebvre, for example, is a short kid who participated in my basketball camps in Fécamp. That's how I met him 15 years ago. Alexis and I have kept in touch because I always saw something in him. In 2014, when he was 23 and had finished college, I asked him to join me on the ASVEL venture. It was his first job. He came on board to manage the event teams on game days, ticketing, etc. When I decided to buy the women's club in 2017, I asked him to work with me on the women's team.

"Oh! No, Tony, I don't want to do women's basketball. It's not the same," he replied.

"Listen up," I told him, "at the end of the year, either you come with me or we shake hands like adults. Basically, you're fired, you'll leave the club!"

"Are you serious, Tony?"

"Yes, I'm serious. This is how I look at it: for everyone who's there, either they agree to combine skills for both teams, or they are no longer part of my club. I have a vision, and I don't want to keep people who don't believe in it."

I gave him an ultimatum, even though he was a close friend. He was shocked but accepted and stayed with the club. Today, he's the women's team's biggest fan. He talks to me way more about Lyon women's ASVEL than the men's team. In May 2019, when I asked him to follow me to the NorthRock Family Office project, which is based in the States and which focuses on advising athletes and artists in managing their assets, he almost cried at the thought of leaving the ASVEL women's team. It's so good to get people to join you in a venture and see how far it takes them. It's priceless to see all the radiant faces when there is a reward at the end.

Winning a title as president of a club is incomparable to winning four NBA titles and the championship of Europe title as a player. As president of a club, you choose everything from A to Z. As a player, you're focused on the athletic season, on the team. The cocoon is much tighter, even though I was lucky enough to play for a very familial club in the NBA, which is not the case with most franchises.

When you win as the owner of a club, you're especially happy for everyone who helped make it happen, and proud that they joined the club. For example, after our second title in 2019, Charles Kahudi could have left to earn more money. He chose ASVEL, and he won two championship titles, the first of his career. When we saw each other at the end of Game 5, it was an incredible feeling. Mitrovic, the coach, could have stayed in Monaco, where he was earning more money. He decided to come with us because he thought he had a better chance at winning the title with ASVEL. Those were tough decisions. Paoline Salagnac left Bourges, a legendary women's basketball club, to join us, even though we didn't even participate in the women's EuroBasket in the first year, and she had played in the EuroLeague the year before with Bourges. Valéry Demory, our women's coach who had won two titles in four years with Montpellier, turned down a six-year contract to join us because he believed in our potential. He knows my father. He's known me since I was a baby. He knows what we stand for. Those are good signs. How this club functions is now well known. People know ASVEL is a family.

We're certainly going to make a lot of people jealous. It's normal. Anyone who knows me knows I'm doing what I do for French basketball. How can they be against us? We're doing it for the right reasons. We're good people. I really believe in karma. Some people think of us as a mafia. That's fine. The people who join us see how we are. We're not cheaters.

In fact, we became successful with the club faster than we thought we would. The 2016 champions of France title was a surprise. When I took over the club in 2014, we had considered accelerating things after three years. It happened in the second year. It was an unbelievable sequence of events. How we won the title was a reflection of who we were. For the first time, a team down 2–0 in the finals won three games in a row. That's what made the saga even more magical. I wasn't there for the first two games. I came back and the team outdid themselves, despite Strasbourg being much stronger than us that year.

We had something special. It made my brothers and me laugh. When we go to finals, we win. Or else we don't go. Finals are for winning. I knew very well that one day I'd lose one, but for the time being, we were winning. I feel like I've always outdone myself ever since I was a little kid: I was told I was too short, too skinny, that I'd never make it. I try to pass that mentality on to my team.

I Mean Business

During halftime of the last game of the 2019 finals against Monaco, I went into the locker room to talk to the players. The first half hadn't been good. The atmosphere was heavy and a little dull. In the end, I didn't have much to say, but I just wanted them to relax and play their game. They weren't playing, they were suffering.

"Why are you letting the pressure ruin all the work you've done this year?" I asked them. "Now is the time to give it all you've got and have as much fun as possible. These moments are made for you, for you to outdo yourselves. Don't think of the end result. The result will be what it will be. At the end of the day, if we win or lose, it's no big deal. But play this game, have fun, do what you have to do. The result most likely will happen by itself. We've been first all year, throughout the regular season. We deserve this. We've beaten them five times. Do your job, and don't think about the outcome. Let loose, and whatever happens, I'll be proud of you. But we can't lose like this. They're walking all over us. They don't respect us, and we're giving them the ball."

It was a positive and motivating speech. No comparison to the one I had given during halftime of the French Cup a few weeks earlier, when we won against Le Mans. I was a little annoyed because I thought they were making a mess of things.

Surely my speeches, whether from the second half of my playing career, or now, as the owner of ASVEL or other businesses, still carry a little weight. It probably comes from experience, from the work I've done over the years and the titles I've won. People know I mean business. I can see it in the way people look at me. They're attentive; they listen to what I say. There's not a single basketball player who won't listen to me. I've been in their shoes. I've won finals, I've lost finals. I've been seriously injured. My entire career has prepared me for this part of the game.

Generally speaking, I usually have good relationships with club presidents. Christophe Le Bouille, president of Le Mans, is one example. I love his club. I love what he's done with Le Mans. I also really admire the work of Jean-Louis Borg and Thierry Degorce in Dijon, and not simply because Thierry is a shareholder in Lyon ASVEL Women's. There are also Martial Bellon and Vincent Collet in Strasbourg. It's a structured club. Our clubs are similar, and there's a lot of communication between them. I obviously have a strong emotional bond with Boulogne. I really like the coach, Freddy Fathoux, and now that the club is going to be managed by Boris Diaw and Alain Weisz, and with Mous Sonko coming on board, the bond is going to grow even stronger. I also like the work of Bourg-en-Bresse. Fred Sarre has done a phenomenal job, and Bourg's coach, Savo Vucevic, was Bondy's coach, which was a team I played against at INSEP. We have good neighborly relations with Bourg. Things are also good with Gravelines and Hervé Beddeleem. He's always supporting me, sending me emails and texts to tell me they've got our backs. I went to kindergarten and first grade in Gravelines, so it's a special city for me. I also loved Limoges, with Fred Forte, who unfortunately passed away on December 31, 2017. Since then, I've had much less contact with Limoges. In Pau, I was very close to Pierre Seillant, the emblematic former president of the club, but now things are going very well with Didier Gadou too. In Nanterre, I get along really well with Franck Le Goff, who participated in my camps for years.

The Academy, My International School
Currently, my biggest project is the Academy.

The idea took shape during my basketball camps about 10 years ago. I knew immediately that I wanted to work with youth players. The Academy was born from my desire to improve French basketball and to give back to my country, but it goes above and beyond basketball.

I had to fight for people to stop referring to it as a "training center." The Academy is an international school. It does not have the same structure as ASVEL. The Academy is a separate business with its own shareholders. Yes, the training center is part of the Academy and benefits from the facilities. But ASVEL pays rent. The Academy's focus is primarily social, academic, and professional. We're not trying to produce pro basketball players, far from it. What we want is for the youth to come out of the Academy with a set of skills and the ability to be a productive, happy member of society. That's really my goal.

When I took over ASVEL in 2014, we had already negotiated the court for the Academy with the mayor of Lyon, Gérard Collomb, in Beijing. There was a delegation from Lyon there, and I was there for Peak, my sponsor. I met them at their hotel, and Gérard Collomb and I negotiated the price of the court and the location near Gerland. In the end, the Academy was born in China.

The Academy is not just for basketball players. When I was young and on summer vacation, I didn't want to play basketball. I wouldn't even touch a ball. To stay in shape, the two sports I played most often were tennis and beach volleyball. There was always a tennis court close by, and there were volleyball courts everywhere on beaches. It was easy to stay in shape. That's why I wanted tennis to be part of the Academy. Caroline Garcia, who is from Lyon, and I connected. We'll see where this takes us. We talk often on the phone. She's a friend now, who often comes to support ASVEL. I would really like to do things with her, when she's ready, of course. My goal right now is to set up a unique project in France that is comprehensive and consistent with both clubs and the Academy.

CHAPTER FIVE

My "Private" Life

I'm aware that my life doesn't look like everyone else's. I have two bodyguards who have traveled everywhere with me for a hell of a long time now. Steve has been with me for 18 years, and Victor for 11. Everything happened so quickly for me, and my life became quite overwhelming when I was just 19 years old. I wanted to have someone with me just as a precaution, because you never know what can happen.

I made the decision to hire a bodyguard in the summer of 2002, when I got back from my first NBA season and during my first basketball camp. Nike had set up in the square of La Défense. Energy in the square was very high, and some people grabbed at me. It was impossible to walk down the street without being accosted by fans.

Like many other NBA players, I decided to hire a bodyguard. It was prevention more than anything. Throughout my career, there have only been three or four times when I've had to deal with excessive fans. Mostly it hasn't been an issue, but that may be because I always have Steve and Victor with me. Their presence is a real deterrent.

The need for security is also related to my lifestyle. At the beginning of my career, I really liked going clubbing.

Sometimes you meet drunk people, and you never know how they're going to act. I've seen NBA players get into fights in nightclubs. When you travel a lot, and when you spend time in airports and go to restaurants, people never leave you alone. Having bodyguards around creates peace. It's given me some time to myself, which is important to me given the fast pace of my life.

It was on one of Steve's days off that I came within an inch of losing an eye. It was in New York, in June of 2012, and Axelle and I were hanging out with Thierry Henry at a club called WIP. The club had its own security. But that night, Chris Brown and Drake got into a fight over Rihanna. Bottles started flying. I was trying to protect Axelle and a piece of glass flew into my eye.

A few hours later, we were on a plane for Paris. I barely slept. I still had a little alcohol in my system, and I didn't really realize there was glass in my eye. My eye was bothering me a bit. I couldn't stop scratching it during the flight. I felt like I constantly had something in it. I mentioned it to Axelle when we arrived at the airport, and we decided to go directly to the ER.

After the doctor examined my eye, he told me I would have to undergo emergency surgery within the hour, because there was a chance I could lose my eye otherwise.

I couldn't believe it. I didn't even have time to call the Spurs to get a second opinion. Luckily I hadn't broken the piece of glass when I was rubbing my eye on the flight. It could have shattered and the injury would have been a lot more serious.

The operation took two hours. They saved my eye, but I had to spend 10 days in the hotel in a completely dark room. Axelle had to put four or five different eye drops in my eye every two hours. The recovery was difficult and inconvenient. Axelle turned into a nurse deluxe. She stayed with me in the dark the entire time. We watched TV for hours. I had a bandage over my eye, and it absolutely couldn't come into contact with the slightest ray of light. We stayed in the dark and ate with only the light from the TV on.

Afterward, there were checkups every two weeks to monitor the scar. Then the Spurs flew me back to the United States and sent me to a specialist in Atlanta to see if I could play in the London Olympics a few weeks later. The specialist didn't want me to play. He thought it was risky. If I were to get hit or take a ball or a finger in the eye, I could have permanent damage. It was still fragile, but it had healed, and I ultimately decided to play anyway with protective goggles.

Luckily for me, nothing happened. It was a strange series of events, starting with what seemed like an innocent night at a club. I sued the nightclub and won, obviously. The experience didn't make me want to go out less, but from then on I always had at least one of my bodyguards with me.

It's definitely hard to explain to people why Steve or Victor comes with me to the bathroom. It's precisely when people see you all alone, in those vulnerable moments, that they try to approach you or talk to you. Sometimes I just want to be left alone. I am always in the public eye, and having Steve and Victor there has become normal. They're part of the family. I don't even notice it anymore. They know everyone. My parents and brothers are surprised when I show up without them. I can go to bed, and my dad will go have a drink with Steve and Victor.

I never complain about this kind of life. I'm still as happy as ever. Being constantly surrounded by people is the price of success. When I'm in the public eye, and the evening is meant for pictures, autographs, and meeting fans, I have no problem with it, and I'm really patient. If I have to take pictures with everyone all night, I'll take pictures with everyone. But if I need an hour to myself, I inform Steve and Victor, and they know what to do. Sometimes they're the ones who get into it with people—not me. That happened once in China, in particular. The fans are more aggressive there, but Steve and Victor are used to it.

Eva Who?

When I met Eva Longoria in 2004, I didn't know who she was. *Desperate Housewives* was new to television. It wasn't yet the global success it would quickly become. So I didn't know who she was. After a game, someone came to tell me she wanted to talk to me.

I said, "Eva who?"

She got to the locker room, we talked for a while, and we hit it off. We didn't spend the evening together but decided to see each other again. Our relationship happened little by little.

In the beginning, I never thought I would be immersed in the world of *People* magazine and movie star fame. Eva wasn't yet the star she was going to become. No one could have predicted that. At the time, how many people become stars in Hollywood from a TV show? You could count them on one hand. I was going out with a normal girl who was an actress in a TV series. That's all. It's not like I had met Julia Roberts and went back home at night and said, "Hey, Dad! I'm going out with Julia Roberts." When I met Eva, *Desperate Housewives* had only been out for two weeks. It was later on that it became a global phenomenon. I watched Eva become a Hollywood star. In the end, we grew up together.

A few months later, in 2005, I became an NBA champion for the second time and *Desperate Housewives* started winning awards everywhere. The same thing happened in 2007: I landed my third NBA title, and *Desperate Housewives* was sweeping every award show. We were both young and both moving up in our respective careers. We were excited. Everything was new, and we would say to ourselves, "Come on, we're going to make it!"

We never really lived together. She was in Los Angeles, and I was in San Antonio. She would come back and forth about every two weeks. In the summer, we would try to spend more time together, but sometimes she had to film, and I had the French national team. Not so easy. She would come see me with the French team when she had a little time. It was more a long-distance relationship than shared life.

When her series started becoming really successful, I was pulled into a world that wasn't mine. I was there to support Eva. I watched and observed. She helped me choose my clothes for galas and red-carpet events. She was really attentive to that. Obviously, our relationship made an impact with the Spurs. Eva's family is from San Antonio. Tim Duncan would joke around in the locker room and sometimes call me "Mr. Hollywood."

I took a private jet for the first time to visit Eva in Los Angeles. At the time, I spent a lot of time in airplanes. I had so much energy. I never rested. I didn't need a lot of sleep and did back-to-back games and public appearances. The

Spurs let me live my life, because Pop knew I was serious. He had met Eva. He knew it was a real relationship and not just a short-term girlfriend. Once he knew that, Pop did everything to make it work. Sometimes he would let me leave earlier to take a plane or would allow me to meet up with the team a little later. He did a lot of things to help make my relationship work. Not all NBA franchises would have reacted this way. The Spurs were really family-oriented. For example, with the Spurs, wives and fiancées were allowed to fly with the players, which was not allowed during my final year, in Charlotte.

Life in Hollywood

I had gone to a few celebrity parties. But what surprised me the most was that Hollywood people were just as impressed by basketball players as we might have been by them.

In the summer of 2004, in Paris, during the world premiere for *Collateral*, the movie starring Tom Cruise and Jamie Foxx, Tom Cruise's sister came up to me.

"Tom would really like to meet you," she said.

"Me? Really?"

"Yes, he's obsessed. He knows all your stats!"

At the time, I was already an NBA champion. I was rather intimidated. It was Tom Cruise, after all. I had seen all his movies. Then, he came out with my stats. He knew everything about me. It was crazy. I understood then that it's not a one-way street, that athletes can also inspire movie stars. When I met Will Smith or Denzel Washington, I realized that they were fans of mine just as I was a big fan of theirs. I knew all of Will Smith's movies, and he knew how many times I had been an NBA champion and All-Star.

Going to the Oscars or walking up the steps in Cannes didn't particularly affect me, simply because it had never been my dream. Winning titles, being an All-Star, those were my dreams. But I was part of the scenery. In 2007, I was an All-Star in Las Vegas. Eva was in the first row with my little brother. Next to them were Mary J. Blige, Jay-Z, and Beyoncé. The crème de la crème who came to see the NBA. My little brother couldn't get over it. He was beside himself.

"Do you even realize? Did you see who I was next to?"

"I see them all the time…now."

Of course, I realized I was in another world, but it was as if I was part of the family. We could be at our house in Los Angeles and decide to play a game with Jennifer Lopez and the other actresses from *Desperate Housewives*. In fact, it became my day-to-day. They were our friends. It's just that they happened to be famous! We would go eat with David Beckham and his wife. Every evening it was something different.

Eva would say to me, "Hey, it's been a long time since I've seen Sheryl. I want to see her. Can we invite her over on Sunday?"

"Sheryl who?" I replied.

"Sheryl Crow."

"Oh, okay. No problem!"

That was our life. I never felt caught up in a whirlwind. We were NBA champions and I was doing my thing on the court. Sure, I will admit that the first six months I was starstruck. I would meet celebrities and say, "Wow!" It's always weird when you're used to seeing someone on TV and suddenly see them in real life. No matter who it is, even if you're not a fan, it's still mind-blowing. Through game nights and dinner parties, we quickly formed normal friendly relationships. When I met Leonardo DiCaprio, who was really nice, it was kind of like I was talking to a work colleague.

Trying My Hand at Music

As I've mentioned, even though my parents were separated, they were always there for me. In their own ways, each of them shaped and influenced me. For example, my mother instilled curiosity and the desire to discover other worlds. Very early on, I wanted to become familiar with the business world. But I was also drawn to film and music.

In 2007, I released an album, *Tony Parker*. The single "Balance-toi" was No. 1 in France for two weeks, and I wasn't too far off from having a gold record. People like to say that my musical venture was a failure, but I don't see it this way at all. For me, it was a breath of fresh air at the right time. I met wonderful people, and even today, I still come across people who know my music and the lyrics by heart. My women's team sang one of my songs and sent me a video of it for my birthday.

In the beginning, I had signed on for three albums with TF1. Unfortunately, the other two albums didn't work out. Making music wasn't compatible with my sports career. They wanted me to go on tour in the summer. I had done three TV appearances and a concert in Lyon. I couldn't keep up that pace. I had to choose between the French national team and a music career. I made my choice. I explained to the people at TF1 that I was committed to the French national team. There was no way I could go on tour and keep playing basketball.

In the end, I only made one album. However, I had spent a ton of time on it. I worked in a studio in San Antonio. I went there almost every night after practices and home games. Since Eva didn't live with me, I had quite a lot of free time, and I worked on my sound and the writing on the side. I loved that world, and I met wonderful people during that time. I worked with a producer named Skalp to make the album. I renamed him "Skalpovich," as a nod to Popovich. Like my coach, Skalp was disciplined, strict, and very meticulous: "No, let's start again, Tony. Again! Redo it like this. Redo it that way." I worked on the writing with Éloquence. I featured Jamie Foxx, Fabulous, Booba, Soprano, and Don Choa from the Fonky Family. My friend, Cut Killer, also gave me a decent amount of advice so I could really understand the music world.

In February of 2006, we did a concert during the All-Star Game in Houston. It was one year before the album came out. Of course, it could have been a lot better. It was the beginning. We had a lot of things to learn. We arrived on stage really late, but in that world, no one is ever on time. The musicians take their time. They're relaxed. It's nothing like the basketball world.

I learned a lot that night, and it was useful for the following concerts. A year later, when my album came out, when I did the show *Hit Machine* on M6 and my concert in Lyon, I was better prepared. I performed about a half hour on stage in Lyon, which was half my album. There were a lot of people there, a lot of teenagers. The crowd was very young. It was nice. After the album came out, I did two or three concerts, three or four TV appearances, and three videos.

Today, I mainly listen to classical music and rock 'n' roll instead of rap. I won't get back into music. Between my family, my kids, and my life as company head, having a career as an artist wouldn't be manageable. It's not possible.

The Fast Lane

Our wedding at the Château de Vaux-le-Vicomte in 2007 was Eva's world, not mine. I think we sold the exclusive story of our wedding to *OK* magazine for $2.4 million. Eva wanted a big wedding, and I had no problem with that. I wanted to make her happy. I told her, "Go ahead, you're in charge." Selling things to magazines is her world.

She and I had reached a high point of fame. I was NBA champion for a third time and the best player in the Finals. I was at the very top of my game. She was on top with her TV show. You don't refuse offers like that. It enabled us to pay for everyone's trip and even to give some money to a foundation.

There were 350 guests. She had nine bridesmaids and I had nine groomsmen, which was a nod to my jersey number. Eva has three sisters, and she didn't want to choose between her friends and her sisters, so we decided to have nine and nine. That way everyone was happy.

We had a huge party. It was an unforgettable night. Having a party like that at the Château de Vaux-le-Vicomte doesn't happen every day. They had opened up a lot of rooms for us that are typically closed to the public.

Those seven years with Eva were a whirlwind. Life in the fast lane. We were both on incredible upward-moving career paths. We were two kids who were fulfilling their respective professional dreams. We were so into it. She never missed any of my playoff games. She was there for my 2005 and 2007 titles, and for all the important games with the French national team. She was there for all my important moments. Everyone who thought it wasn't a real relationship was sorely mistaken. Yes, her career might have put us in the spotlight, but mine did too. A lot of people follow the NBA. It's a war machine, just like Hollywood.

The Divorce

The story of our separation is between her and me. Only we know exactly what happened. I don't have to justify myself to anyone.

It's never easy when a relationship ends, especially when it's public. Some people wanted to take advantage of the situation to make money. You name it, someone said it. The media even wrote on the cover of a magazine that I had given her an STD.

It wasn't easy for my family, especially for my mother, who cried when she read all of that. So many people wanted to take advantage of us. They will say anything and everything in that sort of situation. The only thing you can do is make sure your family and friends know the truth, and let life carry it away. Ride out the storm.

I still had to manage my career and be good on the court. What's pretty crazy is that, in mid-December of 2010 when everything came out, I was voted NBA player of the week. In that moment, I told myself that the only thing I could control was being good at basketball.

At the end of the day, if people think I'm a bad person, I can't do anything about it. I wasn't going to answer each magazine and each comment on the Internet. I have the ability to put the details of my personal life aside when I need to focus and be good on the court. That's always been one of my biggest strengths. As soon as I enter the arena and set foot on the court, that's the only thing that matters. I've always been this way.

The divorce wasn't going to change how I played. In fact, it never affected any of my performances. Not one of them. If I had to choose a character trait that was a deciding factor in my game or my career, it's my mind. Some players are more talented than me. They shoot better, are more technical or athletic, but if there's one area where I dominate, it's with my mindset. It's easy to make shots during practice or even in the first three quarters, but when you have to be on in a critical moment, that's a different ballgame. Throughout my entire career, I've almost always felt that I've had a good game at the right time.

The divorce was complicated between Eva and me because we didn't wanted to hurt each other. We were sad. That's why we stayed in touch for a long time. We even wondered for a minute if we were making a mistake and if we should give it another shot. We always supported each other, and there was no resentment when we left each other. That is proof of love and mutual respect.

I really loved Eva. It was a real relationship. We even tried to have kids. It didn't work out. Our relationship was complicated by our schedules and the physical distance that often separated us. In the end, what happened, happened. I'm not allowed to talk about it or give the reasons why our relationship ended. Both of us agreed contractually to never talk about it publicly.

Eva and I haven't had any contact since 2014, the year I married "Ax."

Axelle

A few months after the divorce, I was celebrating my birthday in New York with Thierry Henry. That's the night I met Axelle.

She was a journalist in New York. She did a little of everything and wrote about several different fields: technology, biology, and fashion, to name a few. At that time, I wasn't looking for a relationship. My marriage had just ended, and Axelle was also recently divorced. Neither of us was ready for something serious. I definitely liked meeting her, but I wasn't looking beyond a fun evening. It happened progressively, over time. I was still in touch with Eva at the time, so I wasn't thinking I could be serious with Axelle.

After three months of talking a lot and getting to know each other, we tried something more serious. It was 2011, the year of the NBA lockout. The season didn't start up again, and I decided to go play with ASVEL for a month or two while the NBA came to an agreement about how to start the season. I suggested that Axelle come with me to Lyon and try living together: "Let's try France, and if it doesn't work out, at least you'll stay there, and it would be pointless to move all your stuff to San Antonio."

Lyon was a test for us. It was our first time living together. I didn't have my house in Saint-Germain-au-Mont-d'Or yet. I had a big suite in an extended-stay hotel. My chef, Cliff, came and stayed in the room right next to ours, and he prepared meals for us every day. Ronny Turiaf, who had also decided to play for ASVEL during the lockout, was in the upstairs apartment. We ate every meal together.

Time was moving on, and neither of us dared bring up the critical question: was she going to come with me to San Antonio? That is, until the NBA announced that they had reached an agreement. The season would start back up on December 25. We decided to try San Antonio, and she came home with me. It was the beginning of our life in Texas.

Our first son, Josh, was born on April 30, 2014. We got married that summer. The wedding was at our house. There were no journalists or cameras, and there were around 100 people there. The celebration lasted one week. A lot of the guests came from France, and we weren't going to have them come in for a weekend. There was a different activity planned each day. For example, I rented out SeaWorld for my guests one day.

David Robinson, my old teammate and center for the Spurs, married us. He had become a pastor after retiring. David and I are really close. He was delighted when I asked him to marry us.

When Eva and I got divorced, David was one of the people I confided in the most. He was really there for me, always attentive, and really supportive. When I met Ax, he was one of the first people I introduced her to.

Balance

My family will always be my top priority. I won't be with my club forever. I have to learn how to deal with that. Up until 2018, it was unimaginable that I would miss an ASVEL home final. Yet, during the 2019 finals, I only stayed for Game 1. I watched Game 2, which was in Villeurbanne, on TV in San Antonio because I had to be there for the kids.

There will be big moments for my club that I will have to miss, especially because we want to keep living in the United States. We like our life here, even though we only speak French at home. But now we'll travel back to France often. I'm getting better at balancing home and career. In 2019, in addition to missing Games 2 and 3 for the men's finals, I missed Game 4 for the women's. Life takes care of itself because both teams won after five games, and I was there for two of the title-deciding games.

I've been president of ASVEL for five years. Everyone knows I love my club. If one day I miss a game where we win a trophy, that's just how things work out sometimes. You shouldn't expect to see me at all the games for the club's EuroLeague comeback, either. I'll be absent more often than present. If I make it to eight or nine of the EuroLeague's 34 games, that will be great.

It's Only the Beginning

My retirement still feels really new. I feel good, and I'm handling it well. I'm so passionate about all of my various projects. What we did with both ASVEL clubs was impressive. In 2019, the year I retired, both teams won in style and in front of our fans. We couldn't have scripted a better finish. You can't make that stuff up. That confirms that I made the right choice and that I can still have incredible experiences, just not on the court in a uniform.

I knew I couldn't do it any longer on the court. Could I have played another year with the Lakers? My friends would tell me, "Go to the Lakers. They don't have a point guard." They clearly could have signed me. I knew Danny Green and had the experience they needed. They definitely could have made me an offer. But it would have been strange for me to play my last season with the Lakers and be a champion with them. I would have felt like I was betraying the Spurs.

I'm really, really happy to be retired. I'm going to be able to spend time with my family and have many other wonderful experiences. I'm only 37. It's just the beginning. After what we did with ASVEL in five years, there is so much potential for more. I've done what I had to do with basketball as a player. I don't think I could have done better.

Having kids changes your priorities. You look at life differently. It puts things in perspective and gives you a different point of view. I love being a father, taking my kids to school, and going back to pick them up. My two sons running to me with their backpacks on their backs yelling, "Papa!"—it's priceless. Those are important moments. I know they won't last forever. They won't run toward me and throw themselves into my arms their entire lives. They're going to grow up fast. When they're 12 or 13, they won't care if I pick them up from school. But for now, when they see me at the gate, their eyes suddenly light up. I'm their hero, and for me, it's really important to be there for them. There are so many moments that I don't want to miss out on with them. During the year in Charlotte, I missed a lot of those little everyday moments, and I didn't want to go through that again.

The birth of my first son took place in the middle of the playoffs during the series against Dallas. It wasn't easy. I was with Axelle, and we were watching TV. Around 9:00 PM she said, "Tony, I think this is it. My water broke."

Laughing, I had replied, "No, not now. Are you serious?" I had a game the next day.

"Yes, yes. I'm serious. We have to go."

I grabbed our things and we raced to the hospital. Everything happened really fast. Josh was born at 11:00 PM. It was weird because they had to put her under. I was there in the room, dressed like a doctor, while Axelle was asleep. It was really weird. I was all alone in the room with Josh. I held him in my hands. Then, suddenly, I realized the huge responsibility that was now facing me. I told myself, "You're now responsible for this little being. You have a tiny life in your hands. You can't mess this up."

When Axelle woke up, she hurt everywhere and was still a little out of it. She had trouble registering it. We really weren't able to enjoy and share Josh's arrival until two or three hours later. Liam's birth was completely different. We were both present and part of the experience from start to finish.

I had always wanted to be a dad, but I wasn't in a rush. I thought it would be a little difficult to take on that role in the middle of a professional basketball career. I would never have seen my children. I wanted to have my kids in my thirties, toward the end of my career. I knew I could be there for them then, from the time they were born.

The first summer after my retirement in 2019, we spent a few days as a family in Lyon during the summer vacation. It was nice to be able to fully enjoy my sons. I would wake up in the morning with them and we would eat breakfast, and our schedule for the rest of the day depended on what they wanted to do: pool, zoo, movies, whatever they wanted. A normal life. I was happy to go everywhere with them. During my career, with the NBA and French team combined, there really wasn't a lot of time left for me to enjoy my family and friends. I had about two weeks out of each year to see everyone, and it was my favorite time: spending time with the people I loved.

I'm really family-oriented. I love being close to people. I love unity and shared experiences. I'm ambitious and motivated. I want to do so many things, and I live life in the fast lane. You only have one life, and I'll have the time to rest when I'm 65, with nothing to do but go out on the boat and look at the sea. But now, I want to experience as many things as possible.

A career demands a lot of sacrifices. Mind you, it was all worth it. I have no regrets. Now it's going to be nice to be able to do a lot of different things.

What a Life!

When I started out, French basketball had a very small place in Europe and in the world. People didn't respect us. My motivation was always to show that we knew how to play basketball in France too. That you could be champion of Europe and NBA champions with a French point guard. I never thought of myself as someone who was going to light or lead the way, but rather as someone who was going to help French basketball have a better reputation. I always took the role of basketball ambassador very seriously. A lot of hopes were set on me when my career began, and I took it as a responsibility, without ever asking myself whether I deserved everything that was happening to me or not.

In June of 2019, I sponsored a basketball camp in Pointe-à-Pitre, Guadeloupe. The joy of the people when I landed, and the star welcome they gave me, warmed my heart. I managed to make an impression on so many people on an island that I had never even visited before that day. The same happened in the Philippines in 2016 when incredible fans greeted me. In Guadeloupe, some people told me, "You've made us so happy, so proud. In our minds, you are Guadeloupean!" That kind of thing is impressive and touching.

The way I grew up, having to take care of my brothers from a young age, learning about being a father before even having my own kids, then becoming a point guard and directing teams—all of this makes me believe that I was born to be a leader.

When I announced my retirement, I received a lot of messages that really moved me. When Pau Gasol said that I was the kind of player you only see once a generation, I didn't know he thought that about me. When Zizou talked about legends, although he himself is one, it was strange. When I started my career, I wasn't thinking about becoming a legend. When you finish your career with this sort of praise, you feel like you've succeeded. When discussing French basketball, people will inevitably stop at the Tony Parker chapter, like they did before with Alain Gilles or Antoine Rigaudeau.

I hope there will be many others after me and that I will have managed to influence an entire generation of basketball players who will carve out their own paths. When I look back and try to take stock of everything I've accomplished, the first thought that comes to mind is: "What a life!"

I'm 38 years old. I feel like I've done everything on the fast track. It's almost like I've lived 10 lives. It's been beyond all my hopes, beyond my wildest dreams. Now I want to see the world and go everywhere. My boat will be ready in 2021.